Virtues, Values, and the Very Best You

Susanna Palomares
Dianne Schilling

cover design by Linda Thille

Copyright © 2007, INNERCHOICE PUBLISHING • All rights reserved
ISBN – 10: 1-56499-055-6
ISBN – 13: 978-1-56499-055-6

Experience sheets may be reproduced only in quantities sufficient for distribution to students in those classrooms utilizing *Virtues, Values, and the Very Best You*. All other reproduction for any purpose whatsoever is explicitly prohibited without written permission. Requests for permission should be directed to INNERCHOICE PUBLISHING.

INNERCHOICE Publishing
15079 Oak Chase Court
Wellington, FL 33414

www.InnerchoicePublishing.com

Most of the interventions that have been created to date are based on the very simple premise that you are what you do. And, if you do more of these things, you'll be more of whatever they represent. So how frequently are you kind? How often are you a leader? Keep track of that and measure it all along so you can track your progress.

Christopher Peterson (on the PBS special, This Emotional Life) speaking on a new Leadership training program piloted at the U.S. Military Academy at West Point, and created by Peterson and Martin Seligman

Contents

Introduction 1

Unit 1—Trustworthiness 7
    How To Be Trustworthy 9
    Honesty 11
    Integrity 12
    Promise Keeping 13
    Loyalty 12
    The Big Lie 15
    You Can't Win By Cheating 18
    The Importance of Trust 20
    Let's Work Together 22
    Together Is Better 23
    Depending On Each Other 24
    I Depend On You—You Depend On Me 26

Unit 2—Respect 29
    Respect vs. Fear 30
    A Recipe for Respect 33
    Respected Friends 35
    Role-Play Respect 37
    Respecting Human Rights 40
    The Bill of Rights 42
    The Habits of Heroes 44
    Interview Form 46
    Hands of Respect 47
    The Web of Life 49
    Chief Seattle's Poem 51

Unit 3—Responsibility 52
    Committing to Responsible Behaviors 54
    Who's Responsible? 56
    Our Everyday Heroes! 59
    Responsibility in Action 61
    Responsibility Log 63
    Goal Setting 64
    This Is My Goal 66
    The Blame Game 68

Unit 4—Justice and Fairness ... 70
Liberty and Justice for All ... 72
Dancing to Our Differences ... 74
Creating Our Classroom Constitution ... 76
Resolving Conflicts Fairly ... 78
What Is Prejudice? ... 80

Unit 5—Caring ... 81
Real People Who Care ... 83
Albert Schweitzer, Reverence for Life ... 85
A Caring Project ... 87
My Caring Project ... 89
Friendship Profile ... 92
Giving and Receiving Praise ... 94
Caring Is the Big Story ... 96
The Kindness Book ... 97
Caring and Kindness in the News ... 99
The Link of Kindness ... 101

Unit 6—Citizenship ... 103
The Rules of the Game ... 105
The Trial ... 107
Speak Up for What You Believe In ... 109
A Classroom Campaign ... 112
Debates and Voting ... 114

Unit 7—Reflections ... 116
Sweet Revenge ... 118
Current Events Research ... 122
Being the Very Best Me ... 124
A Game of Ethics ... 126
Ethics Bingo ... 127
Values Affect Decisions ... 128
Situations ... 130
What Would You Do? ... 131
Decision Point! ... 132
Dilemmas by the Dozen ... 133

Unit 8—Service Learning ... 141
A School Service Project ... 143
A Community Service Activity ... 145

Introduction

Education has always attempted to develop good people. Even during periods when teachers were told that they must not teach values, they did anyway. They modeled kindness, caring, and respect; punished cheating, stealing, and lying; rewarded industriousness; and emphasized the importance of good citizenship in the context of a just and fair school community.

Responsible behavior begins with ethical thinking, and helping students to think — to solve problems, make decisions and render judgments — is clearly the job of the school. Along with language, math, science, and art, schools must teach acceptable standards of conduct, and the attitudes and attributes that foster them. Smart is not enough to sustain the principles and belief systems upon which our society is built. Good, the estranged twin, belongs in this picture.

Because to some degree good comes before smart, to consistently do their best work, students must value excellence, even if it's just an excellent grade. Few students can do well in school without work, and work requires diligence. If every child came to school with well developed senses of responsibility, honesty, integrity, and fairness, teaching would be easy. But since, both practically and developmentally, this is impossible, schools are left with no choice but to instill values right along with the other basics. They always have. They always will. The difference is that today many schools are again teaching values deliberately — through the curriculum.

According to Lawrence Kohlberg and others who have done extensive research on moral development, elementary-age children are primarily concerned with their own survival — avoiding punishment and obtaining rewards by obeying the rules. Older children are motivated by the desire to gain approval from others (principally peers) and avoid disapproval. Only at the highest level of moral development are rules interpreted in terms of self-chosen principles (Crain, 1985). The strong influence of the home in preschool years gives way to the broader world of the school and peer group as children enter school. Educators are not usurping a family mandate by teaching moral values; the children carry the mandate with them, right out the door and into the school. They are whole people, and schools cannot deal with their minds apart from their morality.

Knowing that so many children lack role models and caring adults in their lives, and knowing, as a consequence, that society is in real danger, the educational system would be negligent were it not to respond. To some, character education will seem like just one more job added to the teacher's overwhelming list of responsibilities. But it's a critically important job — and somebody's got to do it.

What Values Should We Teach?

Many teachers in classrooms today recall being told never to venture into the values arena under any circumstances. To those teachers, the current interest in character education must seem rather ironic. Does our concern for morality skip whole decades? What happened?

The short answer is this: While trying to meet the educational needs of an increasingly pluralistic society, educators went through a period of several years wherein no one was sure whose values to teach. With so many cultures, languages, and ethnic groups to accommodate, schools thought it best to leave the entire issue of values alone. Developing character was the job of families, supported by their religious institutions. Unfortunately, both families and religious institutions were losing their sway over young people during that same period of time.

Today, educators are not so worried about "whose values to teach." They are acknowledging that every person needs to acquire certain character attributes and be guided by universal moral values — values that unite all people everywhere because they affirm basic human worth and dignity.

Universal moral values underlie the 1948 United Nations Universal Declaration of Human Rights, which calls for:

- life
- liberty
- freedom from personal attack
- freedom from slavery
- recognition before the law and the presumption of innocence until proven guilty
- freedom from torture
- freedom of conscience and religion
- freedom of expression
- privacy, family, and correspondence
- freedom to participate freely in community life
- education
- a standard of living adequate for maintaining health and well being

The Aspen Conference

The activities in this book have been organized around six core universal moral values outlined by a group of twenty-nine youth leaders and educators at what has come to be known as the "Aspen Conference." Meeting in Aspen, Colorado, in July, 1992, the participants of the conference sought to define a brief yet comprehensive list of values that could serve as a "common denominator," uniting not only themselves, but all people and organizations in our society. The six core values are:

- Trustworthiness
- Respect

- Responsibility
- Justice and Fairness
- Caring
- Civic Virtue and Citizenship

The authors of this book have chosen to devote one unit of activities to each of these six core values. Another unit is comprised of activities that give students an opportunity to review the core values and to identify and discuss those that are relevant to a number of typical life situations. In addition, a final section on Service Learning has been included.

What Schools Can Do

Everything about a school reflects to some degree that school's current set of values. The way administrators lead, counselors interact with students, teachers manage their classes, the way grades are awarded, sports programs are administered, and the way hallways and playgrounds are monitored all send moral messages. These messages, picked up by students on super sensitive receivers, significantly affect character development.

Much of what students learn is learned by imitation or modeling. The younger the student, the stronger the impact of models on development. For this reason, the values that you choose to teach should extend to all aspects of school life.

The experiences generated by being a member of the school community are much more character-forming than anything an individual educator can say on the subject of morality or ethics. Ask regularly: "What lessons are being taught by the way our school operates on a daily basis?"

Does your school...
1. have a philosophy statement clearly outlining character expectations for all members of the school community? Is it posted prominently and a visible part of school life? If you are a teacher, do you have a compatible philosophy statement for your classroom?
2. provide all students with clear academic and behavior goals?
3. have a discipline policy that supports the character goals of the school?
4. encourage students to participate in formal school and/or community service projects?
5. have available to students on a regular basis general school service activities, e.g., teacher aides, messengers, tutors, guest greeters, fund raising, school clean up, etc.?
6. have a range of extracurricular activities led by school staff and supported by parents and community, e.g., sports, band, choir, drama, art club, etc.?

Do you...
1. demonstrate character traits and pro-social habits that are supportive of the school philosophy and goals? Do other faculty, administrators, and certified staff also effectively model these goals and philosophy?

2. see a relationship between the way you treat students and the way they treat each other?
3. have an awareness of how small actions model and teach?
4. share concern for the well-being of others — both students and staff?
5. give extra help to students who need it?
6. educate enthusiastically?
7. come to your classes prepared to lead class activities?
8. return students' work in a timely manner?
9. refrain from gossiping or criticizing students, parents, or administrators?

What Educators Can Do

Moral values are already so tightly woven into the fabric of school and classroom life that we no longer see the individual threads. The school environment is rich with values. The question is: which values?

It is who we are more than what we say that builds character in children. Students learn from what they observe and experience in the environment; they develop the values that you model.

All students, and particularly at-risk students, need consistent caring in the form of support and encouragement. They must know that you believe they can overcome obstacles and that you are depending on them to make ethical, pro-social choices.

The Model
- Treat students with love and respect; set a good example.
- Share your moral convictions with students.
- Talk about community service you perform.
- Establish clear academic and moral goals for your class or group.
- Present well-planned lessons.
- Teach enthusiastically.
- Return homework and test papers promptly.
- Don't gossip about students or colleagues.
- Show consideration for other adult staff.
- Go the extra mile for a student who is struggling.

The Words
- State character goals as positive imperatives, e.g., "Be on time," "Treat others fairly," "Do your best work," "Keep your word." Avoid negative wording, such as "Don't be late," "Don't be unkind," and "Never break a promise."

- Teach values directly. Use the words (i.e., trustworthiness, respect, responsibility, caring, etc.), write and define them, identify the behaviors in which they are embodied, and have students practice those behaviors.

The Environment
- Help students know each other, respect and care about each other, and experience a sense of full inclusion in the group.
- Through cooperative learning, teach children to help each other and work together.
- Display pictures, portraits of worthy individuals, posters, and quotations that reflect the high moral purpose and goals of your class.
- Teach values in conjunction with parents and community.

The Management
- Use the creation and enforcement of rules as opportunities to foster moral reasoning.
- Instill civic values by holding class meetings to discuss problems that arise.
- Involve students in decision making and shared responsibility for making the classroom a positive place to learn.

The Skills
- Teach a decision-making process that encourages students to make conscious choices from among alternatives that have been examined not only for their relative effectiveness in achieving a stated goal, but for their moral consequences.
- Teach skills of listening, communication, assertiveness, problem solving, conflict resolution, and refusal/resistance.
- Give students many opportunities to make choices.

The Academics
- Use academic subjects as vehicles for examining ethical issues.
- Foster academic responsibility and regard for the value of learning and work.
- Encourage moral reflection through reading, writing, and discussion.
- Give students opportunities to respond to moral issues.

How to Use This Book

As mentioned previously, the activities in *Virtues, Values, and the Very Best You* are grouped into eight topic areas or units. The first six correspond to the core values, or "pillars of character," developed by the delegates at the Aspen Conference on character education. The seventh is a summary unit, designed to review and reinforce the concepts presented in the other six. The eighth is a Service Learning unit.

The activities within each unit are arranged in a logical and, to some extent, developmental sequence. However, in most cases you are not required to implement the activities in the order presented. In those rare cases where two activities are linked, the directions so indicate. The great majority of activities are completely independent and capable of standing on their own.

The activities in the summary unit will probably have the greatest impact if they are implemented after the students have examined each of the six core values in some depth. Keep in mind, however, that this unit houses a number of stories and dilemmas. By all means take the liberty of dipping into those at any time. Simply adjust the discussion questions to the readiness of your students to deal with various concepts.

Additional modifications should be made to suit the ages, ability levels, cultural/ethnic backgrounds, and interests of your students. You will know best how to maximize the appropriateness and impact of each experience, so please take those liberties.

At the conclusion of each activity, you will encounter a list of "Discussion Questions." Discussion questions are provided to help you involve students in thinking about and summarizing the learnings derived from a particular activity. They promote moral and ethical reasoning, the use of higher-level thinking skills, and internalization of knowledge and skills. When planning for implementation, always allow plenty of time for debriefing and discussion.

References:

Crain, W. C. (1985). *Theories of development* (pp. 118-136). Upper Saddle River, NJ: Prentice-Hall.

United Nations. (1948). *Universal declaration of human rights*. Adopted and proclaimed by General Assembly resolution 217A(III) of 10, December, 1948.

Unit 1
Trustworthiness

The activities in this section deal with four components of trustworthiness: Honesty, Integrity, Promise-keeping, and Loyalty. To be worthy of trust, students need to understand these values and behave in accordance with them. When you care deeply about the same values — naming, discussing, modeling, and supporting them consistently — much of the teaching will already be done. Here are some guidelines:

Honesty. Give students honest answers. If you don't know or aren't sure, admit it. If you don't think it is appropriate to talk about a subject or if you must withhold information for some reason, say so and explain why. Expect students to tell the truth and do their own work. Don't tolerate cheating, trickery, or deviousness.

Integrity. Demonstrate your beliefs through your behavior. Stand up for what you think is right and speak out about what you think is wrong. Model commitment and courage. Help students verbalize their beliefs by creating an ongoing forum on values.

Promise-keeping. Keep your word. Return homework and test papers on time. If you promise to seek out a piece of information or locate and read a particular book, do it. Likewise, follow though on suggested field trips and special activities, even if the logistics prove difficult. Expect students to complete their work on time, return borrowed items in good condition, and keep their commitments.

Loyalty. Show your support for everyone in the school community. Don't gossip about or criticize students, colleagues, or parents behind their backs. Never participate in rumor mongering. Attempt to stop the spread of rumors and gossip among students as soon as you become aware of them. When students are protective and supportive of one another, point out that they are being loyal and are thereby earning trust.

How To Be Trustworthy

Purpose:
To explore the components of trust-worthiness and brainstorm ways in which those components can be demonstrated in school, home, and the neighborhood.

Materials:
copies of the experience sheet for each team, paper and pencils, chalkboard or whiteboard and writing implements

Procedure:
Write the word *trustworthiness* in large letters on the board. Ask the students if anyone knows what trustworthiness means. Invite volunteers to share their ideas. Incorporating any definitions the students offer, explain that trustworthiness means to be worthy, or deserving of someone's trust or confidence. If you are trustworthy, people can count on you. You can be depended upon to keep your promises, to be honest, to do what you know is right, and to be loyal to those who trust you.

Tell the students that there are four components of trustworthiness: *honesty*, *integrity*, *promise-keeping*, and *loyalty*. Write these four words on the board, and in your own words, give a brief description of each. For example, you might say:

Honesty *is accomplishing or earning something fairly, without cheating or stealing. It also means telling the truth.* ***Integrity*** *is being true to your beliefs, or living by your values. In other words, integrity is doing what you believe to be right.* ***Promise-keeping*** *is just like it sounds — keeping your promises and agreements.* ***Loyalty*** *is being true to those who trust you and depend on you. For example, a loyal friend is willing to say and do things for you publicly. A loyal American publicly stands up for or defends this country and its government.*

Divide the class into eight groups of three or four. Assign one component of trustworthiness to each group, making sure that every component is assigned twice. In other words, two groups will be working on honesty, two on integrity, two on promise-keeping, and two on loyalty.

Pass out the appropriate copy of the experience sheets to each group. The groups working on honesty will receive the Honesty sheets. The groups working on integrity will get the

Integrity sheets, etc.

Distribute writing materials, and ask the groups to brainstorm ways in which their component of trustworthiness can be demonstrated in school, home, and the neighborhood (or community). Using the experience sheets, have them write an action plan which explains how their component can be carried out and supported in each of those places.

When the students are finished brainstorming, ask the groups with the same component to meet briefly and share their ideas. Next, gather the whole class together for sharing. Make a copy of this chart on the board.

	School	Home	Neighborhood
Honesty			
Integrity			
Promise-keeping			
Loyalty			

As the groups share their ideas, invite them to fill in their portion of the chart.

Tell the students that it is now time to develop and implement a personal action plan. Have the students each choose one component that they would be willing to practice for two weeks. Have them write their action plan for the selected component on a clean sheet of paper, using the same sentence pattern that the groups used. Ask the students to keep a daily journal describing specific things they did to support their action plan. Remind them to explain how the component was supported by each behavior. Share journal entries at the end of the two weeks. Conclude the activity with a summary discussion.

Discussion Questions:
1. *What difficulties did you have carrying out your action plan? What was easiest about it?*
2. *What would life be like if no one demonstrated the components of trustworthiness?*
3. *What did you learn about your own behavior from this activity?*

Honesty

We can demonstrate honesty…

…in our school by _____

_____

_____

_____

_____

_____

…in our homes by _____

_____

_____

_____

_____

_____

…in our neighborhoods by _____

_____

_____

_____

_____

_____

EXPERIENCE SHEET

Integrity

We can demonstrate integrity…

…in our school by _____

_____

_____

_____

_____

…in our homes by _____

_____

_____

_____

_____

…in our neighborhoods by _____

_____

_____

_____

_____

Promise Keeping

We can demonstrate promise keeping…

…in our school by _____

_____
_____
_____
_____
_____

…in our homes by _____

_____
_____
_____
_____
_____

…in our neighborhoods by _____

_____
_____
_____
_____
_____

EXPERIENCE SHEET

Loyalty

We can demonstrate loyalty…

…in our school by _____

_____

_____

_____

_____

_____

…in our homes by _____

_____

_____

_____

_____

_____

…in our neighborhoods by _____

_____

_____

_____

_____

_____

The Big Lie

Purpose:
This activity uses stories and dramatizations to help students experience and understand consequences (including feelings) that result from lying.

Materials:
copies of the experience sheet, *The Big Lie*, for each student

Procedure:
Distribute copies of the experience sheet to each student. Ask the students to follow along as you read the story aloud.

When you have finished reading the story, ask the students to help you sequence the events in the story. Create additional dialogue by talking about what Suzie and the other characters might have said in each scene and why. Next, ask for volunteers to act out the story.

After the first group of students has dramatized the story, ask a second group to role-play the same story. Explain to the actors:

We're going to do this role play a little differently. Sometime during each scene, I will say, "Freeze." When you hear that word, hold your positions and stop talking. I will walk among you and tap different actors on the shoulder. When you feel a tap, tell us what your character is thinking and feeling at that moment. I may tap just one person, or I may tap several during each of these "freeze" periods. Continue with the role play when you hear me say, "Resume."

Have several groups of volunteers act out "The Big Lie." Allow one group to act out the sequence of events uninterrupted before adding the "freeze-resume" technique. Conclude the activity with a summary discussion.

Discussion Questions:
1. *How do you feel when you know that someone has lied to you?*
2. *If you frequently lied about yourself and your accomplishments, how do you think other people would react if they found out?*
3. *Do you think that lying can become a habit — something a person does without thinking? If so, how can that habit be changed?*
4. *What would life be like if you couldn't trust anyone to tell the truth?*
5. *How do you feel about yourself when you lie? ... When you are truthful?*
6. *Why should we make truthfulness a habit?*

EXPERIENCE SHEET

The Big Lie

Suzie sat excitedly at breakfast. She couldn't eat fast enough. Neither could her mom and the aunts and uncles she was visiting for the summer. There was a big fair in town and, today, they were all going to attend it. In her mind Suzie could already see the clowns, feel the thrill of the rides, smell the cotton candy and popcorn, and hear the barkers crying, "Knock over just three ducks and win a fabulous toy," or "Step right up and let me guess your weight." When the family was finally ready, Suzie's mom said to her, "You may choose one present for yourself at the fair and I will buy it for you." Suzie couldn't wait to see all of the displays of toys so she could make her choice.

At the fair, Suzie was dazzled by so many beautiful things. As she strolled in front of the booths, she narrowed her choices to a beautiful heart-shaped ring and a soft, cuddly teddy bear. Oh, what a difficult choice! Suzie really wanted them both. At last Suzie told her mom that she wanted the ring, so her mom bought it for her. As they walked around other parts of the fair, Suzie admired the ring on her finger, but she kept thinking of the teddy bear. Then she had an idea. Without anyone noticing, Suzie slipped the ring in her pocket.
Just before stopping for lunch, Suzie cried, "I've lost my ring!" All the family looked around on the ground, but the ring was gone. Suzie's mother felt so sorry for her that she offered to buy her another one. Suzie sniffled, "No, I want the teddy bear." So her mom took her to the booth with the teddy bear and bought it for her. Suzie was delighted that she had fooled her mom and family, and had both presents.

EXPERIENCE SHEET

When Suzie sat down for lunch with her family, she reached in her pocket to check if her ring was still there. Satisfied that the ring was safe, she pulled out her hand. However, the ring accidently came out with her hand and fell on the ground. When the family saw the ring drop to the ground, they knew what Suzie had been up to. They knew that she lied about the lost ring. "You lied to us," her aunt said severely. "How could you have done such a thing?" her mom said as she stared at Suzie in disbelief. "What a bad girl you are!" an uncle scolded.

For the rest of the day, the family acted very cool toward Suzie. She felt awful. She wished she hadn't lied. Her behavior ruined the day for her and her family. Suzie vowed to herself that she would never lie again, no matter how difficult it might be.

You Can't Win By Cheating

Purpose:
To examine the consequences of cheating and to express new understandings through art.

Materials:
chart pad, drawing paper, art supplies, and writing implements

Procedure:
Begin by asking the students: Do you know what cheating is?

Discuss the meaning of cheating, inviting the students to share their perceptions. Add to their ideas by explaining that cheating is getting something in a dishonest way. Ask the students to think of some examples of cheating in school. List their suggestions on the board, adding ideas of your own. The list should include:
—Copying answers from someone else's paper instead of doing your own work.
—Erasing someone's name from a paper and putting your own name on it.
—Taking the teacher's answer book and getting answers to an assignment.
—Getting someone else to do your work for you.

Have the students form groups of three or four. Explain that their task is to brainstorm as many reasons as they can think of why cheating is wrong. Have them focus on the possible effects, or consequences, of cheating in school.

Give each group a sheet from the chart pad and a colored marker. Ask them to select a scribe to record their ideas in large lettering on the chart paper. Allow 5 to 10 minutes to complete the task. When time is up, ask one member from each group to report to the whole class. Post the lists around the room.

If the following "reasons why cheating is wrong" are not included on the student lists, discuss them with the students while recording them on a separate list of your own. Post this list also.
- You lose the teacher's trust that you will do your own work.
- If you cheat in school, you may find it easier to cheat outside of school.
- You will lose your self-respect and pride.
- Cheating is a lie because it causes people to think you know more than you do.
- Cheating may lead to other forms of lying.
- Cheating is not fair to students who are honest.

- If you get into the habit of cheating when you are young, you will find it easier to cheat when you are older.
- Cheating is taking something that you haven't earned, and may lead to other forms of stealing.

Announce that the students are going to have an opportunity to express one of their ideas about cheating in poster form. Distribute the art materials. Suggest that the students choose one "reason why cheating is wrong" from a posted list and try to express that idea in as few words as possible, combining the words with a picture or symbol to complete the poster. For example, the words might read:

✔ **Choose to Cheat? Lose Self-Respect!**

✔ **Cheating is Lying.**

✔ **Cheating: Unfair to Others!**

✔ **Cheat in School? Cheat Out of School!**

✔ **Young Cheaters Become Old Cheaters.**

When the posters are finished, invite the students to share them with the class. Then display the posters on a bulletin board in the school auditorium or library under the heading, "Cheating Is Wrong Because..."

Conclude the activity with discussion.

Discussion Questions:
1. *How would you feel if someone cheated on a test and got a better score than you?*
2. *How would you feel if someone took your work and put his/her name on it?*
3. *How does cheating hurt the community? ...the country? ...the world?*
4. *How does cheating hurt the cheater?*
5. *How do you feel about yourself when you cheat?*
6. *Why is it hard to trust someone who cheats?*

The Importance of Trust

Purpose:
By making agreements and fulfilling them, the students experience and then analyze factors involved in trust-building.

Materials:
a safe grassy area, such as a playground or park, that is secure from hazards and open enough to provide good visibility (for you)

Caution: Choose a safe environment where you can see all students at all times. If an appropriate outdoor area is not available, move furniture and equipment out of the way and conduct the activity indoors, limiting the number of partners on the floor at any one time.

Procedure:
Begin this activity by discussing the meaning of trust. Ask the students what it means to "trust another person" or "be in someone's trust." Make sure you cover the following concepts:
—depending on
—relying on
—putting yourself in someone else's hands
—having confidence in
—keeping agreements
—expecting an outcome (trusting that an expected outcome will occur)

Ask volunteers to share examples showing how people put their trust in others, e.g., children depend on parents to provide them with enough to eat and a safe home; a parent trusts an older child to watch a younger sibling while the parent is making dinner.

Explain to the students that they are going to participate in a two-part activity in which partners work together to build trust. In your own words, give these instructions:

One of you will close his or her eyes, pretending to be sightless, and the other will guide the sightless person around the playground. When you are the guide, you must make two or three agreements with your partner before beginning the walk. These can be promises concerning safety, speed, kinds of movement you will be performing, or warnings about approaching changes in terrain. For example, you might state, "I agree to warn you when we are about to go up hill or down, or when I want you to slow down. I also agree to tell you what you will be touching before you touch it." Another example might be, "I promise not to make you walk into any holes, touch anything dirty like someone's old garbage, or make you bump into anything." As a guide, you must lead your partner around the area safely, while providing opportunities for your partner to touch different objects, listen to sounds, and smell various aromas. <u>*You are to be very careful and must never lead your partner into anything that might be dangerous.*</u> *You may talk to each other during the walk.*

Ask the students to choose a partner or assign pairs, as necessary. Allow 5 to 10 minutes for the walk. When the time is up, blow a whistle or otherwise signal the partners to return to a central location. Direct them to change roles, and have the new guides make their agreements before starting the second walk.

After both walks are completed, bring the group together and debrief the two walks.

Discussion Questions:
1. *What were some of your experiences while you were either the blindfolded person or the guide?*
2. *Did your guide live up to his/her agreements?*
3. *Did your guide's performance help build or break down trust?*
4. *How did you feel while depending upon another person?*
5. *If your guide hadn't fulfilled his/her responsibility, what might have happened?*
6. *What did you learn about trust from this activity?*
7. *How can we build trust with each other in class? ...in school? ...at home?*

Variation:
Older students may enjoy another movement activity called the "Trust Circle." Have eight to ten students form a tight circle. Ask one person to stand stiffly in the middle with arms folded snugly across his/her chest. Then have one of the circle members reach out and hold the middle student by the shoulders while that student leans backwards. Finally, direct the circle members to pass the middle student around by the shoulders while his/her feet remain in center of the circle. Repeat the exercise, giving every student an opportunity to be in the middle. Be sure to monitor and control the activity carefully, ensuring the safe and respectful treatment of every student.

Let's Work Together

Purpose:
To explore and describe the benefits of cooperation and trust.

Materials:
one copy of the experience sheet, *Together Is Better*, for each student, chalkboard, and chalk

Procedure:
Write the word *cooperate* on the board. Ask the students what it means to cooperate with another person. Accept all contributions, jotting key words and phrases on the board. Attempt to agree upon a simple definition of the word.

Remind the students of specific occasions when you have asked groups of two or more to work together to complete a task or assignment. Ask them to think carefully about what they accomplished and how they went about it. Then ask, "What did you gain by working together cooperatively?"

Again, accept all contributions. Through questions and discussion, help the students identify the following potential benefits of working cooperatively with another person:
- When people work together, they save time.
- When people work together, they think of more solutions to a problem.
- When people work together and they all do what they say they will do, trust develops.
- When people work together, their solutions are more creative.
- When people work together, they have fun.
- When people work together, they do a better job.

Distribute the experience sheets. After going over the directions, give the students a few minutes to complete the sheet. When everyone has finished, have the students share what they have written in small groups. Facilitate a culminating class discussion.

Discussion Questions:
1. What are some ways that you cooperate with others at home?
2. Why is it important to cooperate when working with others?
3. What happens when one person in a group is uncooperative?
4. If you had an uncooperative person in your group, what could you do?
5. What happens when someone in a group doesn't follow through on his or her responsibility?
6. Once you lose trust by not being responsible, how easy or difficult is it to regain that trust?
7. When you lose someone's trust, can you get it back? …How?

EXPERIENCE SHEET

Together Is Better

In the space below, write two or three sentences that describe what cooperating means to you. Below are some words that you might want to use. Use other words, too.

share	team	together	listen	talk
compromise	win	work	enjoy	support
help	think	laugh	accomplish	

Cooperating means _____

_____

_____

_____

In the space below write about a time you worked cooperatively and trusted each other to do what you were supposed to do.

_____

_____

_____

_____

_____

_____

_____

Depending On Each Other

Purpose:
To identify people that students depend on and to describe how they depend on them, and then to describe how a lack of dependability affects others.

Materials:
one copy of the experience sheet, *I Depend On You—You Depend On Me,* for each student chalkboard, and chalk

Procedure:
Begin by asking the students: *How do you feel when someone praises you for being dependable? Have you ever heard someone say, "I'm depending on you?"*

Ask the students to explain what it means to be dependable. Facilitate discussion, exploring various meanings of the term. In the process, read the following scenarios to the students and ask the accompanying questions. Encourage the students to think of all the people who might be affected in each story, and how they would be affected (consequences).

- Sally has a lead role in the school play. Practices are on Monday and Wednesday evenings. Sally is playing with a friend one Monday afternoon and loses track of time. She misses a rehearsal.
  —*Who are the people affected by Sally's absence? How are they affected?*
  —*Do you think the other actors and the director will feel they can depend on Sally in the future? Why or why not?*

- Six people plan a surprise birthday party for one of their friends. They figure out a menu and everyone agrees to bring one dish. Tom is supposed to bring a decorated birthday cake from the bakery, but he forgets to order it. An hour before the party he rushes down to the supermarket and buys a ready-made cake with no decorations.
  —*Who is affected and how?*
  —*If you were one of Tom's friends, would you want to depend on him for future events? Why or why not?*

- Three students are working together on a project for the science fair. They are representing their whole class. On the day of the fair, two agree to come to the auditorium early and set up the display. The third, Lila, agrees to make a chart outlining the steps in the group's experiment. Lila buys only one piece of poster board, and then puts off making

the chart until late the night before. When she messes it up, she has to wait until the next morning to get more poster board and redo the chart. By the time she gets to the auditorium, the judges have already passed her group's display.
—*Who is affected and how?*
—*What could Lila have done differently?*

Distribute the experience sheets. Instruct the students to list people they can always depend on, and describe what it is they depend on them for. In addition, tell the students to describe one thing each of the people listed can depend on them (the students) to do.

Have the students share their experience sheets in groups of three to five. Lead a follow-up class discussion.

Discussion Questions:
1. *Are you sometimes responsible for a younger brother or sister? What are your parents depending on you to do?*
2. *How do we depend on each other here in class?*
3. *What are some ways in which people in a community depend on each other?*
4. *Does being dependable mean you can never make a mistake? Explain.*
5. *How does it feel when you depend on someone for something and they do what they said they would do? …don't do what they say they will do?*
6. *How does being dependable affect the willingness of others to trust you?*

EXPERIENCE SHEET

I Depend On You—You Depend On Me

Responsible people are people you can depend on. They keep their promises. They do their best, even when it is hard. They do their duty to others, to the community, and to the country.

Think of people you can always depend on. Then describe one thing each person can depend on you to do.

People I Depend On

Name	I can always depend on this person for...	This person can always depend on me for...

People I Depend On

Name	I can always depend on this person for…	This person can always depend on me for…

Unit 2
Respect

Respect means showing regard for the worth of someone or something. It includes respect for self (self-esteem), respect for others, and respect for the environment, including other life forms. All other varieties of respect are outgrowths of these three. Respecting someone's property, for example, extends from respecting the owner of the property.

Respect is a restraining value. It tells us what not to do. When we urge children to respect each other's privacy, we mean don't interfere or interrupt. When we admonish students to respect school property, we mean don't misuse equipment, don't deface walls, don't damage buildings.

When we teach students to show respect, we prevent them from hurting what they ought to value. If we are completely successful, they will end up valuing that for which they have demonstrated respect.

Other ways to foster respect include:

• Create a democratic classroom environment, in which the rights of all students are respected. Show your own regard for every student, every day.

• Expect students to be polite and courteous. Consistently model the use of "please," "thank you," "excuse me," etc.

• Really listen to the opinions and contributions of students. Make it a rule that students listen respectfully to each other.

• Show your appreciation for diversity. Create an environment in which individual differences are celebrated, and where all students feel included and interdependent.

• Teach students a simple decision-making process and encourage them to use it. Respect their ability to make decisions for themselves. Serve as their advisor and consultant.

• When students have difficulty understanding how their behavior affects others, suggest that they apply the classic test of reversibility. Ask them: Would you want to receive this kind of treatment?

Respect vs. Fear

Purpose:
To help students define the moral value of respect, and distinguish respect from fear.

Materials:
the words *Respect*, and *Fear* written on two signs (one word per sign); masking tape; writing materials for the students; a recording of Aretha Franklin's "R-E-S-P-E-C-T" (optional)

Procedure:
Without preliminaries, intrigue the students by asking them to listen, and maybe even dance, to a song. Play Aretha Franklin's famous version of "R-E-S-P-E-C-T" (if available).

After enjoying the recording, engage the students in a brief discussion about the song and its meaning. (Franklin wants her man to treat her right and literally spells out what that means to her.)

Show the students the sign with "Respect" written on it. Without defining the term, ask them, "Do you appreciate being treated with respect?" Listen to their responses before commenting:

The word "respect" may mean different things to different people. People sometimes experience other feelings and mistake them for respect. Here's one of those other feelings:

Show the students the sign with "Fear" written on it and ask them: *Have you ever heard people say they respected someone, or a group, when they really feared the person or group? If so, tell us about it, but please don't mention any names.*

Listen to the responses of the students, clarifying the distinctions between respect and fear. Then, explain the activity:

We're going to get good at distinguishing between respect and fear. This means we will become clear about which one is which. I'm going to place the "Respect" sign on one wall, and the "Fear" sign on another wall. Then I'm going to read a short description of a person or situation. After I finish reading, get up and go stand under the sign that describes how the first person in the story really feels about the person or group I read about. Don't worry if other students select a different sign than you do. You have a right to your opinion and we respect it. If you change your mind and move to another sign we will respect that, too.

Post the signs on two different walls. One by one, read the situations described at the end of the activity. After each reading, give the students time to stand under the sign that best describes the feelings of the first character in the story. As soon as all of the students have decided where to stand, ask each group why they selected that sign, and listen to their responses.

After everyone has shared, direct the students to form teams of about four members each. Distribute writing materials and explain:

Now it's your turn. Talk with the members of your team and work together to come up with a situation in which someone either respects or fears another person or group. Then select a recorder to write a description of the situation. Later, we will listen to each team's situation and decide which emotion, either fear or respect, the person in the story is feeling.

After the teams have developed their situations, have each team's recorder read the situation to the class. Then, have the class stand and go to the sign that best describes how the person in the story feels. Allow a spokesperson for the team that developed the situation to ask the students on what basis they made their selections. Lead the class in a culminating discussion.

Discussion Questions:
1. *What does it mean to have respect for another person? ...for oneself? ...for the environment?*
2. *If you respect a person, do you also respect that person's property? Explain your reasoning.*
3. *What are some examples of "common courtesy" (saying please, thank you, excuse me; waiting one's turn, etc.) and how do they relate to respect?*
4. *How do we learn to respect others?*
5. *Why is respect for others necessary in a civilized society?*

Situations

How does Bill feel?

Kim and Bill have lived next door to each other for years and they know each other's family well. Kim lives with her parents and younger brother in a nice house. Recently her father was laid off from his job and the whole family has been trying to help. Kim's mother has taken on an extra job and Kim is doing her best to take her mother's place at home whenever she can. She keeps things neat and clean and often prepares food. Bill is disappointed one day when he asks Kim to go bike-riding with him and she says she is too busy at home. But the main feeling Bill has for Kim is _____? (RESPECT)

How does Sarah feel?

Sarah is reading the story of Huck Finn by Mark Twain, the part about how bad Huck's Dad treated him. At the start of the book, Huck's Dad comes back to town suddenly and, when he finds Huck, beats him up and drags him away from the foster home where he's been living with two nice old ladies. Huck's father is very drunk and later tries to kill Huck, but doesn't even remember it the next day when he wakes up. Sarah knows how she would feel about her father if he were like Huck's. She would feel _____? (FEAR)

How does everyone feel about Terry?

Terry is a big kid who likes to be in charge. When Terry joins a team, he always becomes captain. When he works on a project with other kids, he gets first pick of the jobs that have to be done. If Terry says it's his turn to use the computer, everyone else steps aside. Nien, a new student, can't understand why Terry always gets his way. She asks Phil, "Why do you always do what Terry asks?" to which Phil answers, "I don't know, we just do." But Nien thinks she understands. She guesses that what everyone feels for Terry is _____? (FEAR)

How does Sergio feel?

Sergio watches the other boys in his neighborhood pick on a new kid named Sam, who is the shortest sixth grader he's ever seen. While this is happening, Sergio notices Sam looking at the boys in a serious way. He doesn't yell or cry and he doesn't even show fear, although Sergio knows that in Sam's place he would be afraid. Finally Sam says, "Okay, okay, you guys. I'm new. I'm short. But I'm not a bad guy to have around. After you get to know me, you'll like me." This surprises the boys so much they start to laugh. They tease Sam some more and then they leave him alone. How do you suppose this causes Sergio to feel about Sam? (RESPECT)

A Recipe for Respect

Purpose:
This activity helps students gain a clearer understanding of respect by discriminating between behaviors that are respectful and disrespectful and by generating examples of their own.

Materials:
five descriptions of respectful behavior and five descriptions of disrespectful behavior written on ten tagboard strips about 30 inches long (see below), one blank tagboard strip about 30 inches long per student, and one magic marker for every four students, one large mixing bowl labeled "Respectful Actions," a wooden spoon, and one wastepaper basket labeled "Disrespectful Actions"

Procedure:
In preparation for this activity, write brief descriptions of respectful and disrespectful behaviors on the tagboard strips. As much as possible, use examples of behaviors that you have observed among the students in your class. Randomly mix the tagboard strips together and place them upside down in a stack. Here are some examples:

Respectful behavior:
- Greeting people when they walk in the room.
- Looking at people when they talk to you.
- Listening to someone who is speaking to you.
- Offering to share your lunch or snack with someone.
- Saying I'm sorry after bumping into someone.

Disrespectful behavior:
- Not saying hello to someone who has greeted you.
- Laughing at someone who has stumbled.
- Borrowing something from someone without permission.
- Walking away from someone who is talking to you.
- Not saying I'm sorry after bumping into someone.

Introduce the activity by showing the class the mixing bowl (twirl the wooden spoon around in it) and the wastepaper basket. Point out the labels attached to these items, and have the students read them with you. In your own words, explain:

We have been talking about respect — what it is and what it isn't. Today, we're going to create a "Recipe for Respect." Probably the best way to understand respect is to know which <u>actions</u> are *respectful and which are disrespectful. I have some descriptions of both kinds of actions here (hold up the 10 tagboard strips you prepared) and I'm going to need your help in deciding whether an action is respectful or disrespectful. If it's respectful, it should go into our bowl, the "Recipe for Respect," and if it's disrespectful, it should go out with the trash.*

Hold up one of the tagboard strips and read it together. Ask the class where it should be placed and why.

Distribute the nine remaining tagboard strips to nine students. One by one, allow the students to read their strips to the class, drop them into the bowl or trash basket, and explain their judgments.

Divide the students into teams of four, and provide each student with a blank tagboard strip. Distribute the magic markers. Explain the assignment:

Now it's your turn to come up with actions that are respectful and disrespectful, and write them down on tagboard strips. Your team should generate examples of two respectful actions and two disrespectful ones. When all of the teams have written down their actions, every student will come to the front of the class, show and read one example, place it in the bowl or the trash basket, and explain why you put it there.

As the students generate their statements, circulate and assist with composition, spelling, etc. Then facilitate the sharing and selection process outlined above, making sure each student explains his/her reasoning.

Ceremoniously take the "Disrespectful Actions" out to the school dumpster and let the students dump them in. Prepare a bulletin board in the classroom or cafeteria with the banner, "A Recipe for Respect." Allow the students to post the "Respectful Actions" under the banner. Have them draw and post pictures of cooking utensils and food items to add a clever note.

Discussion Questions:
1. Why do we want to "throw away" disrespectful actions?
2. What would our world be like if all people were respectful of one another?
3. Do you think people should be required to earn respect, or do you think all people are entitled to respect? Explain your reasoning.

Respected Friends

Purpose:
Respect is a critically important ingredient in friendship. This becomes clear to students as they contemplate healthy friendships through art and writing.

Materials:
art materials of your choosing; writing materials

Procedure:
Prior to beginning the activity, write the following words on the chalkboard:
trustworthy
loyal
responsible
honest
kind
considerate
sensitive
generous
fair
caring
dignified

Introduce the activity by telling the students about a childhood friendship you had with an individual you greatly respected. Describe the individual using adjectives similar to those listed on the board. Include an anecdote or two to illustrate the character of your friend and emphasize the degree to which this person's actions and attributes caused you to respect him/her. Answer any questions the students have while continuing to illustrate the importance of respect between friends.
In your own words, ask the students:

Does this make you think of someone you really like and respect? Close your eyes and bring someone to mind. (Pause for a few moments.) Perhaps you can think of a time when this person made you proud that he or she was your friend. Maybe you found out how your friend helped someone who needed help, kept a promise, met a responsibility, told the truth when it needed to be told, or stuck up for you. Perhaps you remember a nerve-wracking situation that your friend handled very well, when others might have gone to pieces.

Listen to the students' responses. Then explain that they are going to draw pictures illustrating these friendships. In your own words, explain:

Show something your friend did — an action that caused you to respect him or her. You can put yourself in the picture, too. Perhaps you want to illustrate something very meaningful that your friend did for you. This friend does not have to be your age; he or she can be a family member, someone older or younger than you, even an adult — anyone whom you respect and consider a friend.

Circulate as the students draw, engaging them in conversation about their illustrations. Suggest they consider using cartoon-style speech bubbles to show what is being said.

Distribute writing materials and instruct the students to tell the same story in words. Point to the adjectives on the chalkboard and read them together, urging the students to use any that describe their friend. Tell them to explain who their friend is, how the friendship started, how long it has lasted, and why they respect this person. Give some examples:

I respect Cindy a lot because she is usually kind and considerate to other people. She is always one of the first to be friendly to new kids at school.

I respect Hahn because he is honest and fair, and can be trusted to keep his promises. He promised to help me with fractions and now I'm doing much better in math.

As the students write, circulate and offer assistance and encouragement. Conclude the activity by inviting individual students to read their stories and show their illustrations to the class. Allow the class to ask questions and offer positive comments at the end of each presentation. Make your own positive comment to each child as well. Finally, collect the illustrations and stories and prepare a display including each student's illustration placed above his/her written story, under the banner: "Friends We Respect and Why"

Discussion Questions:
1. What are some reasons we gave for respecting our friends?
2. Do the friends we described show respect for others? What are some of their respectful behaviors?
3. Why is it important to show respect for others?
4. Is it important to you that your friends respect you? ...Why?
5. What did you learn from this activity about how to be a respected friend?

Role-Play Respect

Purpose:
By participating in a series of role plays, the students identify and practice responding to others respectfully in social situations.

Materials:
a container (basket or box) containing role-play directions written on slips of paper (provided at the end of the activity)

Procedure:
Prepare for this activity by copying the role-play directions, cutting out each role play, and placing them in the container.

Announce that the students are going to role play the use of respectful behaviors — actions that demonstrate courtesy and high regard for others.

Invite twelve students to draw role descriptions from the container; tell them to read the descriptions silently and not to share them with anyone. As you do this, explain to the class that you are casting the roles for three different scenarios. Point out that each role description is numbered 1, 2, or 3, and that these designations indicate in which scenario the actors will participate.

Have the three casts meet for 15 minutes to plan and rehearse. Tell them to prepare two scenarios: one showing disrespectful behaviors in the situation, and the other showing respectful actions.

Direct the students who do not receive acting parts to be careful observers of the dramatizations. Tell them that they will have opportunities to demonstrate additional respectful behaviors following the positive versions of the scenarios.

Meet briefly with each team to clarify its scenario.

Moderate the presentations, giving enough advance information about each scenario to enable the audience to understand what is going on. To maximize comparisons, have each team present its respectful version immediately following its disrespectful version. After the respectful version, ask audience members to come forward and demonstrate additional respectful actions that could be used in situations like the one dramatized. Facilitate discussion following each role play.

Discussion Questions:

At the end of each role play showing disrespectful behavior, ask the students:
1. *What happened in this role play that was disrespectful?*
2. *What caused the disrespectful behavior?*
3. *How did the disrespectful behaviors cause others in the scenario to feel? How would you have felt in a situation like this?*

At the end of each role play showing respectful behavior, ask the students:
1. *What respectful actions did you observe in this scenario?*
2. *Did the respectful behaviors require any special skills? What were they and how can they be learned?*
3. *How did the respectful actions make others feel? How would you have felt in this situation?*

Scenario #1: "Introductions." A student is in the grocery store with his/her mother or father. They encounter the child's teacher. The teacher and the parent have never met each other. Since the child knows both of them, the respectful action would be to introduce them to each other in a friendly way.

Role-Play Descriptions for Scenario #1:

> #1 Play yourself. You are with one of your parents at the grocery store.

> #1 Play the teacher of this class, shopping for groceries.

> #1 Play the mother or father of a student. You are with your child at the grocery store.

Scenario #2: "Greetings, Thank You's, and Goodbyes." One student is having a birthday and the student's parents are giving him/her a party. One-by-one, three invited students arrive. The scenario should include what happens as each child arrives and what happens after the party is over and each child leaves. Respectful behavior includes warm greetings, sincere thank you's and friendly good-byes.

Role-Play Descriptions for Scenario #2:

> #2 Play yourself arriving at a birthday party.

> #2 Play yourself arriving at a birthday party.

> #2 Play yourself arriving at a birthday party.

> #2 Play yourself. It's your birthday and your parents are having a birthday party for you.

> #2 Play a mother hosting a birthday party for your son or daughter.

> #2 Play a father hosting a birthday party for your son or daughter.

Scenario #3: "Disagreements." Two students are writing a story together and decide to use the word *license*. Both students insist that they are spelling the word correctly. Since a dictionary is not available, they go to another child who is a good speller and ask for help.

Role-Play Descriptions for Scenario #3:

> #3 Play yourself. You and a friend are writing a story together, and want to use the word *license*. You incorrectly spell LISENCE, but believe you have spelled the word right.

> #3 Play yourself. You and a friend are writing a story together and want to use the word *license*. Your friend incorrectly spells LISENCE. You know it is wrong and say so.

> #3 Play a student who is a good speller. Two of your friends are writing a story and can't agree about how to spell the word *license*. They come to you for help.

Respecting Human Rights

Purpose:
Through research and creative team presentations, the students explain the history and intent of five basic human rights and the U.S. Bill of Rights.

Materials:
a copy of *The Bill of Rights of the United States of America* (Provided), five dictionaries, art and writing materials

Procedure:
Prior to leading this activity, write the words *Liberty, Justice, Autonomy, Privacy,* and *Dignity* on the chalkboard.

Introduce the activity by asking the students what it means when someone has a "right" to something. Listen to their responses, paraphrase as necessary to clarify meaning, and express your appreciation to each child who responds. Then look up the word "right" in the dictionary and read the applicable definition to the class. In your own words, explain:

We have been learning a lot recently about respect. Rights and respect go hand-in-hand. When you respect someone, you do not knowingly violate, or hurt that person's rights in any way. You protect his or her rights, and you object if anyone tries to take them away. People who truly respect you do the same for you. Furthermore, if you respect yourself, you stand up to anyone who tries to violate or take away your rights, unless doing so endangers you. But let's be sure we know what we're talking about. What exactly are our "rights?"

Point to the five words written on the chalkboard and read them with the students. Explain:

These are five basic human rights. The first two are mentioned in the Pledge of Allegiance. People in many other countries have these rights too, but as Americans each of us is <u>guaranteed</u> these rights, which means that the government promises not to violate them or take them away from us. In addition, our laws help prevent anyone else from violating them or taking them away.

Have the students form six teams. Assign one of the human rights listed on the board to the first five teams. To the sixth team, assign the U.S. Bill of Rights. Explain that each team is going to create a way to explain the meaning of its assigned right to the rest of the class. The sixth team is to study the Bill of Rights and explain to the class how it came to be written and what it means. Suggest that students use art, music, drama, or any other method to get their message across. One possibility is to show what happens when the right is violated and when it is respected.

Help the teams get started. Distribute dictionaries to five of the teams and the copy of The Bill of Rights to the sixth. Give the teams time to complete research, and to plan, create, and practice their presentations. Circulate as the teams work, consulting with them and assisting as needed.

As the teams make their presentations to the class, help them only if absolutely necessary. (In some cases you may need to serve as a narrator or the initiator of discussion.) Encourage the class to ask each presenting team questions following its presentation. After all of the teams have made their reports to the class, bring closure to the activity by asking the questions below.

Discussion Questions:
1. *When you respect someone's rights, what are some ways you almost always show it?*
2. *When you respect someone's rights, what are some things you never do to that person?*
3. *Should the rights of every person automatically be given full respect or should individuals earn that respect? Explain.*

The Bill of Rights

The Conventions of a number of the States having, at the time of adopting the Constitution, expressed a desire, in order to prevent misconstruction or abuse of its powers, that further declaratory and restrictive clauses should be added, and as extending the ground of public confidence in the Government will best insure the beneficent ends of its institution;

Resolved, by the Senate and House of Representatives of the United States of America, in Congress assembled, two-thirds of both Houses concurring, that the following articles be proposed to the Legislatures of the several States, as amendments to the Constitution of the United States; all or any of which articles, when ratified by three-fourths of the said Legislatures, to be valid to all intents and purposes as part of the said Constitution, namely:

Amendment I

Congress shall make no law respecting an establishment of religion, or prohibiting the free exercise thereof; or abridging the freedom of speech, or of the press; or the right of the people peaceably to assemble, and to petition the government for a redress of grievances.

Amendment II

A well regulated militia, being necessary to the security of a free state, the right of the people to keep and bear arms, shall not be infringed.

Amendment III

No soldier shall, in time of peace be quartered in any house, without the consent of the owner, nor in time of war, but in a manner to be prescribed by law.

Amendment IV

The right of the people to be secure in their persons, houses, papers, and effects, against unreasonable searches and seizures, shall not be violated, and no warrants shall issue, but upon probable cause, supported by oath or affirmation, and particularly describing the place to be searched, and the persons or things to be seized.

Amendment V

No person shall be held to answer for a capital, or otherwise infamous crime, unless on a presentment or indictment of a grand jury, except in cases arising in the land or naval forces, or in the militia, when in actual service in time of war or public danger; nor shall any person be subject for the same offense to be twice put in jeopardy of life or limb; nor shall be compelled in any criminal case to be a witness against himself, nor be deprived of life, liberty, or property, without due process of law; nor shall private property be taken for public use, without just compensation.

Amendment VI

In all criminal prosecutions, the accused shall enjoy the right to a speedy and public trial, by an impartial jury of the state and district wherein the crime shall have been committed, which district shall have been previously ascertained by law, and to be informed of the nature and cause of the accusation; to be confronted with the witnesses against him; to have compulsory process for obtaining witnesses in his favor, and to have the assistance of counsel for his defense.

Amendment VII

In suits at common law, where the value in controversy shall exceed twenty dollars, the right of trial by jury shall be preserved, and no fact tried by a jury, shall be otherwise reexamined in any court of the United States, than according to the rules of the common law.

Amendment VIII

Excessive bail shall not be required, nor excessive fines imposed, nor cruel and unusual punishments inflicted.

Amendment IX

The enumeration in the Constitution, of certain rights, shall not be construed to deny or disparage others retained by the people.

Amendment X

The powers not delegated to the United States by the Constitution, nor prohibited by it to the states, are reserved to the states respectively, or to the people.

The Habits of Heroes

Purpose:
Through interviews and research, the students identify heroic individuals, and describe their actions and the qualities and characteristics that lead to heroic deeds.

Materials:
access to a library with encyclopedias and biographies of heroic figures, current issues of magazines such as *Time* and *Life* writing materials, a copy of the experience sheet, *Interview Form*, for each student

Procedure:
Introduce this activity by sharing with the class two or three descriptions of the lives and deeds of heroic individuals, some more well-known than others. These might include: (1) a biography located in the school library of a famous hero or heroine, (2) A description of a noted person's life from an encyclopedia or web site, or (3) A popular magazine, such as *Time*, or *Life*, with a story about an exceptional, but perhaps rather "ordinary" person. In your own words, explain:

Almost everyone is interested in people, alive or dead, who have done something unusual. If the unusual thing they have done inspires our admiration and respect, we often call them heroes or heroines. They interest and inspire us; we talk about them and write about them so their stories won't be forgotten. Let me show you some examples.

After showing the class each book and/or article, explain that you want each student to "play detective" by conducting an investigation. Their task is to interview a parent, grandparent, other relative, teacher, neighbor, or friend. They should start by explaining that the interview is for a school assignment, and then ask: "Who is one of your most respected heroes or heroines — someone alive or dead whom you admire and respect?" Instruct the students to listen and take notes, being careful to find out what the hero did (or does) that is so impressive.

Once the students have a verbal account of the hero, direct them to find written information in magazines or books at home or in the library. Tell them to find out what makes this person so remarkable and deserving of admiration and respect.

Have the students prepare a written report of their findings. From the written report, ask them to develop a brief oral report. Both reports should include:
- a description of the impressive actions of the hero or heroine
- the identity of the interviewee who first mentioned this person
- the student's feelings about the hero/heroine after completing the research and writing

Pass a copy of the experience sheet out to each student and have them use it to prepare their final report.

After all of the students have given their oral reports, ask several questions to facilitate a summary discussion, writing the responses of the students on the chalkboard.

Discussion Questions:
1. Most (or all) of the people we've reported on are famous in some way. Can an ordinary person be a hero? Explain.
2. What kinds of actions were our interviewees most impressed with?
3. What qualities and characteristics caused our heroes to do the things they did?
4. How do people get these qualities and characteristics — are they just born with them or do they learn them as they grow up?
5. What do heroes teach us?

EXPERIENCE SHEET

Interview Form

The person I interviewed is: _____
_____

The hero or heroine is: _____
_____

The actions that make this person a hero or heroine are: _____
_____
_____
_____
_____
_____
_____

My thoughts about this hero or heroine are: _____
_____
_____
_____
_____
_____
_____
_____

Hands of Respect

Purpose:
To have students identify respectful actions and describe an incident in which they demonstrated respect.

Materials:
art paper, scratch paper, and pencils, colored markers, or crayons

Procedure:
Begin by asking the students to think of things that people do to show respect for one another. Focus on small courtesies like greeting a person, saying please and thank you, holding a door, letting someone go first, and shaking hands. Tell the students:

I've heard that some coaches insist that their players shake hands with the members of the opposing team after every game, regardless of whether they win or lose. Why would a coach do that? What message does the coach want to send the other team? What do the players learn by doing this?

After the students have had a few minutes to talk about this display of respect, announce that they are going to participate in an activity about respect, but in this activity instead of shaking hands, they'll draw hands.

Have the students form dyads. Distribute the paper and pencils.

Instruct the students to take turns tracing each other's hand on a sheet of art paper. Point out that the drawing they end up with will not be of their own hand, but of their partner's hand. When they have finished tracing, explain the next step (in your own words):

Interview your partner to find out how your partner shows respect for other people. See if your partner can remember a specific time when he or she said or did something that demonstrated respect for a particular person. Take notes on your scratch paper. Then let your partner interview you. When both of you have finished, use what you've learned to illustrate the tracing of your partner's hand to show the respectful things your partner does. Use letters, symbols, pictures, and other decorations. Your illustration can symbolize lots of respectful actions, or it can tell the story of one particular incident. Decide who will be the first interviewer and get started.

Make available the art materials. List the following questions on the board to assist the students during their interviews:

Interview Questions:
- How do you show respect for other people?
- Can you remember a specific time when you did something for another person that showed respect? What happened?

When the students have finished their drawings, direct each dyad to form a circle with two other dyads. Instruct the students to go around the circle and introduce their partner by showing their hand drawing and describing their partner's respectful actions.

Lead a culminating class discussion.

Discussion Questions:
1. A picture of two hands shaking is often used as a symbol of mutual respect and peace. Why do you think that is?
2. What are some other ways of showing respect that we included in our drawings?
3. If you offered to shake someone's hand and that person refused, what would you think?
4. Why is it important to show respect for others?
5. What would life be like if no one showed respect for anyone else.

The Web of Life

Purpose:
Students will create a symbolic expression of their connectedness and describe positive qualities that they respect in one another.

Materials:
a large ball of string; a copy of Chief Seattle's poem for each student

Procedure:
Have the students sit on the floor in a large circle. Determine which student's birthday is closest to the present date. Confer on that student both the ball of string and the honor of starting the activity. Instruct the student to grasp the end of the string and hold it while throwing the ball across the circle to another student.

Next, direct the student who threw the ball to say something positive about the student who catches it. In your own words, elaborate:

Look directly at the student who catches the ball of string, and describe one thing you respect and appreciate about that person. If you think he or she is friendly, humorous, athletic, helpful, loyal, musically talented, has nice hair, is a math whiz, or has a great smile — say that to the person. The "catcher" must accept the positive statement and can say "thank you" or "thanks," but nothing else. Holding onto the string, the catcher then throws the ball to another person in the circle and repeats the process. When it's your turn to throw the ball, you can aim at a specific person, but you must accept and speak to whomever catches the ball. With our throwing skills, we should be able to include everyone, with no repeats, the first time around.

Make sure the students continue to hold onto their portion of the string, keeping it fairly taut. When everyone has had at least one turn to throw and catch, and a web has been formed that connects everyone in the circle, tell the students that you would like to read them a poem written one and a half centuries ago by a Native American chief. Read the poem slowly.

Give the students an opportunity to respond to the poem and its meaning. You may want to read it a second time. Then, direct the group to stand up carefully. Admire the web for a few final moments before asking the last person (the one holding the ball) to move around the group and rewind the string. If you have made handouts of the poem, distribute them. Otherwise, direct the attention of the students to the poem copied on the board. Refer to the poem while leading a final discussion.

Discussion Questions:
1. What does this poem say about respecting the earth and everything on the earth? Does that include people? Explain.
2. What is meant by the words, "All things are bound together. All things connect?"
3. In what ways are all of us in this class connected?
4. How are we connected to the rest of the school? ...the community? ...the nation? ...the earth?
5. What is meant by, "Whatever he does to the web, he does to himself?"
6. Can you describe an example showing how what one person in our class does affects everyone else?

Chief Seattle's Poem

All things are bound together.
All things connect.
What happens to the Earth
Happens to the children of the Earth.
Man has not woven the web of life.
He's but one thread.
Whatever he does to the web
He does to himself.

—Chief Seattle, 1856

Unit 3
Responsibility

Responsibility literally means, ability to respond. It is an active value, compelling us to help others, fulfill our obligations, and contribute to the community and society.

Responsibility is also closely related to trustworthiness, in that it implies being dependable, keeping commitments and not letting others down.

Acting responsibly requires taking into consideration the consequences of various alternatives before choosing a course of action. How will everyone involved be affected? Once a decision is made, it means taking responsibility for the outcome, even if the outcome bears little resemblance to what was predicted.

To encourage responsibility in your students:

• Model responsibility by fulfilling your own obligations to the very best of your ability. Present well-planned lessons. Teach with energy and enthusiasm. Give extra help to students who are having trouble.

• Teach a decision-making process that encourages students to make conscious choices from among alternatives that have been examined not only for their relative effectiveness in achieving a goal, but for their consequences.

• Use a similar process to help students solve problems democratically. Require that students consider minority views and attempt to achieve consensus.

• Use cooperative learning to teach children how to work interdependently, doing their part, helping and including others, and sharing responsibility.

• Expect students to be thorough and accurate in completing assignments. Award grades fairly, based on merit.

• Encourage service learning in the classroom by regularly utilizing messengers, monitors, clean-up helpers, and tutors. Encourage students to team up with "homework buddies" and to become participants in cooperative learning projects.

• Give students opportunities to respond to moral issues. Ask them:

—What is the responsible thing to do in this situation?
—Who behaved responsibly? Who didn't?
—Who was responsible for what happened in this situation?
—Would you want to be treated like this? Why or why not?
—Would you want all people to act this way in situations similar to this one? Why or why not?

Committing to Responsible Behaviors

Purpose:
To encourage the students to publicly accept responsibility for positive actions at school and home, to self-report their progress, and to receive acknowledgment for keeping their commitments.

Materials:
descriptions of 10 responsible classroom behaviors written on tagboard strips about 30 inches long; one blank 30-inch tagboard strip per student and one magic marker for every one to four students; three boxes, one labeled, "We all take responsibility," the second labeled, "Some of us take responsibility," and the third labeled, "One person takes responsibility;" self-stick labels; a banner reading, "We Take Responsibility"

Procedure:
Prepare the tagboard strips in advance. Mix the strips together and place them face down on a surface at the front of the classroom. Use the following examples, or list responsible behaviors that are more relevant to your classroom.

Responsible Behaviors:
- Walking into the classroom quietly.
- Trying not to bother others.
- Putting things back where they belong.
- Putting trash in the wastebasket.
- Listening to the teacher or student who is speaking.
- Bringing in play equipment after recess and lunch.
- Cleaning and straightening the bookshelves.
- Erasing the chalkboard at the end of the school day.
- Taking all books back to the library twice a week.
- Distributing and collecting special materials.

Introduce the activity by showing the class the stack of cardboard strips and the three boxes. Read the labels together. Explain in your own words:

We have been learning about a very important kind of action — responsible action. Now we are going to go a step further. Each of you is going to promise in front of the class to do at least one responsible action. I have written some tasks and behaviors on tagboard strips and you are going to have a chance to write some, too. But first let's decide in which box to place each of these actions, and let people volunteer to take responsibility for them.

One by one, show the strips to the children, reading each one aloud with them. Ask the students to decide if the behavior described is something all students should do, some should do, or only one child needs to do. As each behavior requiring total class commitment is read, ask the students to join together and say the words, "I take responsibility to..." and then read in unison the behavior written on the strip. Ask volunteers to accept responsibility for those behaviors that the class agrees require only one or a few students. Ask the volunteers to pledge, "I take responsibility for... ." Jot the name of each volunteer on the back of the appropriate tagboard strip. Place all strips in the correct box.

Distribute the blank tagboard strips and magic markers. Tell the students that you want each of them to think of a responsible behavior to commit to carrying out at school or at home. Brainstorm examples and list them on the board. Ask the students to think about
- responsible behaviors that make the classroom enjoyable for everyone
- tasks and responsibilities that need to be done at schoo
- tasks and responsibilities that need to be done at home and are helpful to parents
- caring for pets responsibly
- taking care of equipment and possessions

As the students take turns using the magic markers, allow them to help each other with wording and spelling. Circulate to lend your own assistance as well.

Have the students categorize these responsible actions into the same three categories as they did the first group. Ask each child to publicly pledge to take responsibility for the behavior described on his/her tagboard strip.

Prepare a display of the responsible actions under the banner, "We Take Responsibility!" Place the strips listing behaviors that everyone committed to in a column down the center of the display area. Make two more columns — one containing the behaviors that require the commitment of several students, and the other listing the behaviors for which one student has volunteered. Around the behaviors in these last two categories, cluster the names of committed students written on self-stick labels.

Facilitate periodic follow-up discussions, focusing on the progress of students in keeping their commitments. Acknowledge and reinforce responsible behavior.

Discussion Questions:
1. *How do you feel when you do the thing you pledged to do?*
2. *What problems have you had keeping your commitment?*
3. *Do you think it helped to make your commitment in front of the class? ...Explain.*

Who's Responsible?

Purpose:
To give students practice in 1) making decisions about who bears responsibility in specific situations and 2) describing alternative responsible behaviors.

Procedure:
Begin this activity by announcing to the students that you have one or two stories to read (or tell) them. Two excellent stories are summarized below.

The Bell of Atri

The king installed a bell in a tower in the Italian town of Atri, and announced to the people that the bell should only be rung when someone felt he or she had been wronged. Through the years, every time the bell was rung, the judges came together to right each wrong. After years of wear and tear, the bell's rope became old, torn, and shortened. This worried the judges, because if a child were wronged, the child would not be able to reach the rope. To solve this problem, a man tied a grapevine to the end of the rope, making it long and strong enough for even the smallest child to operate.

In the hills above Atri lived a man who had been a famous knight when he was younger. He had a great horse that was his best friend and had saved him from many dangers in his knighthood days. But as the man grew older, he became a miser and loved nothing but gold. He sold everything he could for money except his horse, which had grown very old and feeble. The man thought no one wanted the horse, so he turned it out without trying to sell it. The poor horse could barely find enough grass to eat and was slowly starving and freezing from the cold. People ran the horse off and treated it badly.

One day, shortly after the grapevine was tied to the rope of the bell of Atri, the horse was looking for food and wandered near the tower. The horse saw the green leaves on the grapevine and took a bite, which pulled the rope. The bell sounded and it seemed to say, "Someone has done me wrong!" The judges came running and immediately saw the situation: The poor horse was telling the world how it felt in the best way it could. They ordered the old miserly knight brought before them, and made him spend half of his gold on food, a new stable, and a green pasture for his poor old horse.

Icarus and Daedalus

Daedalus was a very famous and clever builder and artist in ancient Greece. King Minos of the nearby island of Crete had a big problem: A minotaur (a horrible monster that was half bull, half man) was on the loose. Minos succeeded in getting Daedalus to come to Crete to build a prison that would hold the beast. Icarus, the young son of Daedalus, went with his father. Daedalus designed and built the prison, but when he and his son wanted to sail back to Greece, Minos imprisoned them in the top of a tower. He wanted Daedalus to be on call to take care of any other problems that might arise.

Being very clever and never giving up, Daedalus came up with a method of escape, which he learned from the sea gulls as he watched them fly. After collecting lots of feathers, he created a huge pair of wings fastened together with string and wax. Then he taught himself to use them. Next, Daedalus made a pair for Icarus, and gave his son flying lessons. Then Daedalus and Icarus waited for the perfect day when the winds would be just right for flying back home to Greece.

When the right day came, father and son prepared to leave, but first Daedalus gave Icarus a warning: "Don't fly too low, because the sea spray will get your wings wet and bog them down, or too high, because the sun's rays will melt the wax. Either way you'll crash. Just stay by me and you'll be fine." As they took off, both were scared, but soon they got used to flying and Icarus in particular became full of joy. He forgot his father's warning and sailed higher and higher.

Daedalus yelled for his son to come back, but Icarus was completely overcome with the urge to get as close to the heavens as he could. Little by little the feathers came off, then all of a sudden the wax melted completely and no matter how much he beat his arms up and down Icarus could not stay aloft; he fell into the sea and drowned. Daedalus, the sad father, finally found his son's body and carried it to Greece for burial. Later he built a temple over the grave in memory of the son he loved so much, who failed to follow his guidance at a crucial time.

After reading (or telling) the stories, engage the students in a discussion concerning who was, or should have been, responsible for what. Help the students recognize three moral lessons illustrated in the stories:
- People are obligated to care for each other and their animals.
- Parents are responsible for guiding their children.
- Children have the responsibility to listen to, and follow, their parent's guidance.

Next, read the scenarios to the students, asking the accompanying questions and facilitating discussion.

Scenarios

1. You and your parents are visiting the home of some relatives or friends. One of the boys in the family, who is your age, throws a rock at his little brother. No adults are around at the time.
 —*Do you have a responsibility to do anything?*
 —*If so, what is the most responsible thing to do?*

2. You enter a store with one of your parents, and see a wallet on the floor. You pick up the wallet and look inside. You see that the wallet contains money. Your parent has not noticed any of this.
 —*Do you have a responsibility to do anything?*
 —*If so, what is the most responsible thing to do?*

3. Your sister begged for a puppy for her birthday and got one. But now it is almost a year later, and she has practically forgotten the dog. She rarely gives him fresh water or feeds or plays with him.
 —*What is the most responsible thing to do in this situation?*

4. Your friend comes up to you before school starts and tells you she didn't do her homework and wants to copy yours.
 —*Who is responsible for your friend's homework?*
 —*What is the best thing for you to do?*

5. Your friend is angry at his sister and his Dad. Yesterday, he got into a fight with his sister, which he says was all her fault, but his Dad punished them both. Today, you are at your friend's house and you are thinking about what happened.
 —*Do you have any responsibilities in this situation?*

Conclude the activity with more questions and a summary discussion.

Discussion Questions:
1. *Imagine that you are the little kid having rocks thrown at him in the first scenario, or the person who lost the wallet in the second scenario, or the dog in the third scenario. How would you feel if no one was responsible enough to care about you or help you?*
2. *Is it always a good idea to help someone who is asking for help? Is helping always the most responsible thing to do?*
3. *How can you tell if a situation is your responsibility?*
4. *Why is it important to know who is responsible for what?*

Our Everyday Heroes!

Purpose:
Through brainstorming, interviewing, photography, and art, the students develop insight concerning the important roles "everyday heroes" (parents, relatives, neighbors, teachers, etc.) play in their own survival and well-being.

Materials:
art and writing materials, a banner that reads: "Our Everyday Heroes: The Responsible Adults We Know"

Procedure:
Begin this activity by conveying its underlying theme to the students. Use a personal example or describe a scene from a story or movie that explains this idea: The people who make the most important positive impact on our lives are the responsible ones who nurture us each day of our childhood — our parents, aunts, uncles, teachers, neighbors, and other significant people. Here is an example:

I want to tell you about a scene I once saw in a movie that I'll never forget. The movie is "The Magnificent Seven," and it's about seven American gunmen who go to a little Mexican town to help the poor people fight off a gang of bandits who are stealing everything they have. The little boys in the town think that the gunmen are great, and make them their heroes. In the scene I remember so well, the boys are telling one of the gunmen that he is so much better than their fathers who are only farmers and not as tough as he is. It shocks them when the gunman gets upset and insists that they have it all wrong. He says that he is a coward compared to their fathers, because he never had the strength or the guts to get married, have children, and work hard every day to feed a family.

That scene caused me to realize how true it is that the real heroes and heroines are the people who work every day in regular jobs, do their best to bring up children even though they might not do it perfectly, and hang in there day after day, month after month, year after year. The real heroes and heroines are "everyday heroes" because they are highly responsible. Without them, where would we be?

Listen to the responses of the students. Discuss the fact that "everyday heroes" are so often taken for granted, yet very deserving of acknowledgment and appreciation. Suggest that the students select a person in their own life and plan to interview that person. Explain that you would like the students to help you create a gallery displaying photos and drawings of "everyday heroes."

Together, brainstorm the contents of an introductory letter. Write the letter on the chalkboard. Later, convert it to a template for duplication. Here is a sample letter:

Dear _____,

Our class has been talking about the responsible adults we know who work hard every day and do their best to help other people whenever they can. We call these people "everyday heroes."

To me, you are one of these important people. Would you help me by allowing me to interview you? These are the questions I would like you to answer:

1. How did you learn to be a responsible adult?
2. What are the best and the worst things about being an "everyday hero (or heroine)?"
3. Who were your heroes and heroines when you were my age?
4. When you were my age, were any of your heroes "everyday heroes?" If so, who were they?

Thank you,

_____

P.S. Will you give me a recent photo? Or may I draw a picture of you for a gallery display at school?

Have the students sign their letters. Encourage them to take notes during their interviews and to take or obtain photos or draw "portraits" of their interviewees.

Facilitate a class discussion regarding what the students learned as a result of their completed interviews. Chart their responses:

Discussion Questions:
1. *How did our interviewees learn to be responsible adults?*
2. *What did they say is the hardest thing about being a caring, responsible adult?*
3. *What are their rewards?*
4. *Who were their heroes (and heroines) when they were your age?*
5. *Did they have any "everyday heroes?" If so, who were they?*

Invite the students to help with the gallery display. Arrange the photos and drawings under the banner, "Our Everyday Heroes: The Responsible Adults We Know." Under each photo/drawing, place a caption with the name of the student interviewer and the "everyday hero."

Responsibility in Action

Purpose:
To have students relate specific examples of responsible behavior and then monitor and describe in writing responsible and irresponsible behaviors for a prescribed period.

Materials:
two or more copies of the *Responsibility Log* for each student; chalkboard and chalk

Procedure:
Begin by discussing the meaning of the word *responsibility*. List the following components of responsibility on the board and ask the students to think of *specific* examples that might fit under each one. Invite them to share incidents from their own experience.

Accountability
- Think before you act.
- Before you make a decision or take an action, think about how it will affect the other people involved. What will be the consequences?
- When you do something wrong or make a mistake, admit it and accept the consequences. Don't blame others or make excuses.
- Give credit to others for their achievements.
- Do what you should do, or have agreed to do, even if it is difficult.

Excellence
- Set a good example in everything you do.
- Do your best.
- Keep trying — don't quit.
- Make it your goal to always be proud of your performance (schoolwork, homework, projects, completed chores, athletic, or other performances, etc.)

Self-control or self-restraint
- Always control yourself.
- Control your temper — don't throw things, scream, hit others, or use bad language.
- Wait your turn.
- Show courtesy and good manners.

Being a good sport
- Win and lose with grace
- Accept congratulations when you win; accept responsibility when you lose.

• Take pride in how you play the game, not just whether you win.

Continue the discussion until the students understand the meaning of responsibility and many specific examples of responsible behavior have been shared. Then announce that, for the next few days, the students are going to keep logs describing actions that are clearly responsible and clearly not responsible.

Distribute the "Responsibility Log" and go over the directions with the students. Explain that the students should write down actions that they know are responsible (doing their best on a homework assignment and completing it on time; admitting when they forget to do a chore; congratulating the other team when they lose a game, etc.) as well as actions they feel *are not* responsible (not paying attention in class, blaming another person, procrastinating on an assignment, etc.).

Announce a date when the completed logs are due. Allow from two to five days, depending on the maturity of your students. Commend (for their responsibility) those students who complete the logs on time.

Before collecting the logs, have the students share their results in groups of four. Finally, lead a culminating class discussion.

Discussion Questions:
1. *Which do you have more of, actions which are responsible or actions which are not responsible?*
2. *What surprised you about the results of your log?*
3. *How do you feel when you take a responsible action? How do you feel when your actions are not responsible?*
4. *In which area of responsibility do you think you need to improve?*

Responsibility Log

For the next few days, pay close attention to your actions. Write down things you say and do that are clearly responsible actions. Also, write down things you say and do that you realize are not responsible actions.

Action	Responsible? Yes or No	Reactions of Others	I Learned

Goal Setting

Purpose
To have students identify behaviors that they would like to eliminate or improve and then write goal statements and plans for achieving change.

Materials:
Responsibility Logs (from the previous activity), one copy of the experience sheet, *This Is My Goal,* for each student

Procedure:
Ask the students to recall the time period during which they kept a Responsibility Log. Suggest that keeping the logs probably made them more aware of their behaviors. Ask: *How many of you identified behaviors during that time that you would like to improve?*

Point out that one of the things a responsible person does is attempt to reduce or eliminate bad habits, change undesirable behaviors, and always strive to improve him/herself. This is done through setting goals, and then achieving those goals, step by step.

Return the Responsibility Logs. Give the students a couple of minutes to review them.

Announce that you want the students to choose one behavior that they would like to improve. That behavior can be one they identified through keeping their log, but it doesn't have to be. Give the students a few moments to think this over and then ask volunteers to tell the class about the behavior they have chosen to work on.

Discuss the concept of goal setting. Explain that every time the students decide on something they want to do or accomplish, they have set a goal, whether they call it that or not. The key is deciding. When they actually do or accomplish the thing, they have achieved their goal.

Distribute the experience sheets and briefly review the directions. While the students are completing the sheet, circulate and help them formulate goal statements.

Have the students share their completed goal statements with a partner. Ask the partners to make a pact to help each other reach their goal — with reminders, encouragement, and questions like, "How are you doing on your goal?"

Informally check to see how much time most of the students have given themselves to reach their goal. Then be sure to check with the class at regular intervals during that time, giving the students a chance to discuss their progress.

Discussion Questions:
1. *What problems have you had reaching your goals?*
2. *How can you solve those problems?*
3. *Why is goal setting part of being a responsible person?*
4. *What can happen if you want to change a behavior but don't bother to set a goal?*

EXPERIENCE SHEET

This Is My Goal

A goal is like a target. It is something you aim for. The clearer your target — the better you can see it — the easier it is to hit. Also, your target has to be within *range*. If it is too far away, you don't have a very good chance of reaching it.

Think of a behavior that you would like to improve. Describe it here:

_____

_____

_____

Now, turn that description into a goal. A goal should say what you are going to do, instead of what you are not going to do. In other words, make it positive! Read the examples, below.

My goal is to:
—do a good job on my homework and turn it in on time
—peacefully eat and talk with my brother/sister at the dinner table
—on weekdays, get my homework done before playing
—tell the truth
—help mom with the dishes at least twice a week, without being asked

Write your goal here:

_____

_____

_____

Is your goal realistic? In other words, is it something you have both the ability and the desire to accomplish? You must want your goal very much, and you must also be able to do the things required to reach it.

EXPERIENCE SHEET

What steps must you take to reach your goal? Do you have to improve your study area? ...stick reminders on your door or mirror? ...ask someone to help you? List the steps below:

Step 1 _____

_____

_____

Step 2 _____

_____

_____

Step 3 _____

_____

_____

Step 4 _____

_____

_____

Step 5 _____

_____

_____

When do you want to reach your goal? Write a target date here:

_____

What reward will you give yourself when you have achieved your goal?

_____

_____

The Blame Game

Purpose:
To have the students explain the importance and benefit of accepting responsibility for their actions and to creatively demonstrate the contrast between blaming and being responsible in specific situations.

Materials:
drawing paper, colored markers, pencils, or crayons, sample cartoon strips clipped from the newspaper

Procedure:
Begin by asking the students how they feel when they get blamed for something they didn't do. Listen to their responses, and then ask: *Have you ever been in a situation where a person has done something wrong or made a mistake, and you know it, but the person denies it?*

Point out that when we deny responsibility for our actions, we are in effect blaming someone else — even if we don't actually point a finger at someone and say "she did it."

Give the students several examples of blaming and elicit many more from them. Here are some possibilities:
- A child with frosting on his/her face denies having eaten a piece of cake.
- A student fails a test and says the teacher is stupid or unfair.
- A man has a car accident and blames his wife because she was talking and taking his attention away from the road.
- A person is late for work and blames the heavy traffic.
- A teenager breaks his mother's favorite vase and says that it shouldn't have been so close to the edge of the shelf.
- A batter keeps missing the ball and claims the pitcher is lousy, the sun is in his eyes, and the spectators are making him nervous.
- A child is caught shoplifting and tells her mother, "The other kids made me do it."

Announce that the students are going to make pairs of cartoon strips, one showing a blaming situation, and the other showing the same situation but with the "guilty" character accepting responsibility in the last frame.

Distribute the art materials and make available a number of sample cartoon strips. Suggest that the students illustrate a situation from their own experience, or one that was mentioned

in the earlier class discussion. Stipulate that each cartoon strip should have at least three frames, showing:
1. the incident (mistake or wrongdoing)
2. the decision concerning what to do (showing fear, guilt, confusion, inner struggle, etc.)
3. blaming/denying or acceptance of responsibility

Students whose situations require additional frames should be urged to limit the number to a maximum of six.

When the cartoons are finished, post them on a bulletin board. As a class, look at and discuss each pair of cartoons, giving praise and feedback to the artist. Spread this process over several days, if necessary, facilitating discussion during each session.

Discussion Questions:
1. *Why is it hard to admit when you are wrong?*
2. *When you make a mess, whose job is it to clean it up? Why?*
3. *Does anyone ever really make you do something? Explain.*
4. *How do we benefit by admitting our mistakes and taking responsibility?*
5. *What are some of the things that can happen if we don't accept responsibility?*
6. *What have you learned from this activity?*

Variation:
Instead of making cartoons (or as an alternative for some students), allow teams to develop two skits, one dramatizing a blaming situation and the other showing the same situation with the character accepting responsibility.

Unit 4
Justice and Fairness

At school, models of justice and fairness are everywhere. Students know whether or not grades are geared to merit and performance. They soon learn which authority figures make judgments impartially, based on evidence, and which are swayed by personal feelings and prejudices. They know who will listen and who will not.

Components of justice and fairness include impartiality in decision making, commitment to equity and equality, openness to information and ideas, use of reason, adherence to due process, and consistent, impartial application of rules, rewards, and consequences.

Specific ways to instill the value of justice and fairness include:

- Create and enforce rules democratically and use infractions of rules as opportunities to foster moral reasoning. Ask: "Do you know what rule you broke?" "Can you explain why the class agreed on this rule?" "Why was what you did wrong?"

- Encourage moral reflection in conjunction with reading assignments and through writing and discussion.

- Teach the skills of conflict resolution and motivate students to commit to solving conflicts in fair, nonviolent ways.

- When moral issues present themselves, ask the students to weigh the justice and fairness of alternative courses of action.

- Make sure your discipline policy supports the development of strong moral values in students.

- To check the fairness of decisions, have students apply tests of reversibility and universalizability. Ask them:

—*Would you expect to receive this kind of treatment in a similar situation and would you consider it fair? (reversibility)*
—*Would you want all persons to be treated like this in similar situations? (universalizability)*

Liberty and Justice for All

Purpose:
To understand the meaning of justice and to find examples of justice in real life.

Materials:
newspapers, white construction paper, colored markers, and pencils or paints

Procedure:
Begin by reminding the students of the last phrase of the "Pledge of Allegiance" which says, "with liberty and justice for all." Ask the students if they know the meaning of the word *justice*. Allow volunteers to share their knowledge and perceptions of what justice is. Explain that justice means that everyone gets equal treatment under the laws of our country. It means giving deserved rewards and punishments impartially. It also means not favoring one person over another or showing prejudice against a person. On a personal level, it means treating people fairly and without prejudice or favoritism. It means respecting each other's differences and acting reasonably toward one another.

Give examples of justice at home, in the classroom, in the community, and in the nation. Share some examples from newspaper articles, and offer some personal examples as well, such as:

- All the children at home must do their chores before watching TV or going outside to play. No one is favored.
- Everyone gets a turn to talk when there is a class discussion.
- If an adult runs a red light while driving a car, that person is breaking the law and, no matter who s/he is, will have to pay a fine if caught.
- Everyone in our country who is accused of committing a crime is entitled to a fair trial.

Distribute art supplies and ask the students to think of an example of justice at home, at school, in the community, or in the nation. Invite the students to draw a picture of that example of justice. Under the picture, have them write the words. "This is an example of justice because..." completing the sentence with a brief explanation of how the picture depicts an example of justice. For example, a student might draw a picture of a child holding up a test with an "A" on it, writing below: "This is an example of justice because an 'A' is earned only by people who get a high score."

When the pictures are finished, invite the students to show them to the class, reading aloud the reason why each is an example of justice. Post the pictures on a bulletin board in the class or in a highly visible location elsewhere in the school. Summarize the activity by asking some thinking questions and facilitating discussion.

Discussion Questions:
1. *What would it be like if the teacher gave good grades only to his/her favorite students and not to everyone who earned them?*
2. *Why is it so difficult for us to treat each other fairly?*
3. *What does it mean to be partial?*
4. *When is it okay to be partial to someone or something? When is it not okay?*
5. *What is the difference between being partial and being prejudiced?*
6. *A popular saying states that "justice is blind." What does that mean? Do you think justice in our country is really blind?*

Dancing to Our Differences

Purpose:
This activity is designed to help the students develop understanding of and respect for individual differences by practicing tolerant behaviors toward each other.

Materials:
chalkboard or whiteboard and writing implements; instrumental musical selections on record, tape or CD; record player, tape recorder or CD player

Procedure:
Begin this activity by asking the students to think about all the ways in which people are the same. Invite volunteers to share their ideas while you list them on the board. Some suggestions might include humanness, basic needs (air, water, food, sleep), ability to communicate, ability to move body parts, and the five senses. Next, ask the students to think of ways in which people are different. The following are possible answers: sex, ages, cultural background, race, language, talents, looks (color of hair, eyes, skin, height, and weight) and disabilities. List these on the board, too. Explain that people are often intolerant of each other's differences and sometimes treat others unfairly because of one or more of these differences. In order to live peacefully together, people must respect each other's differences. In fact, by celebrating differences, people are more apt to enjoy a diverse, joyful, and creative life.

Announce that the students are going to participate in a movement activity in which each person will have an opportunity to creatively express what makes him/her unique and different.

Divide the students into groups of three or four, ensuring diversity in each group with respect to gender, culture, talents, personalities, size, and any other differences you feel are important. Ask each group to discuss their differences and think of creative movements that represent each person's unique qualities. Explain:

Be sure to develop several unique movements for each member of your group. The movements should fit the special qualities of the person. Practice a "dance" or "pantomime" in which each person performs his/her representative movements while the other members of the group hold positions that spotlight or support the featured person.

While the groups are creating their movements, play instrumental music that can later be used to accompany the dances. Invite the students to practice to the rhythm of the music. Circulate and give support and suggestions as needed.

Invite each group to perform its completed dance before the entire class. Be sure to acknowledge and applaud each "performance." Ask the audience to notice how each individual expressed his/her uniqueness and how group members demonstrated their support. After each performance, discuss these observations. Conclude the activity by asking one or more questions and facilitating a summary discussion.

Discussion Questions:
1. *How did it feel to acknowledge and support each other's differences and to have your own differences celebrated?*
2. *How can celebrating diversity, or people's differences, make the world a more enjoyable place in which to live?*
3. *What would the school be like if we were all the same? What would our community be like? ...our nation?*
4. *Why do you think people are afraid of differences? How can such fears be overcome?*

Creating Our Classroom Constitution

Purpose:
To promote moral reasoning and democratic process. To create ownership of rules and a moral obligation to follow them.

Materials:
chalkboard or whiteboard and writing implements; pencils and writing paper

Note: Although this activity is best done at the beginning of the school year, it is also effective during the year as a means of reevaluating classroom rules and assessing the need for new ones.

Procedure:
Introduce this activity by asking the students, "Why do we have rules in school?" Encourage a discussion concerning the purpose of rules. Possible answers might include:
- Rules help keep order.
- Rules help to ensure individual and group safety.
- Rules help create an atmosphere for learning.
- Rules provide guidelines for everyone to follow.

Then, ask the students, "What would school be like if we had no rules?" Expect answers like:
—"Tough kids would always get what they wanted."
—"It would never be quiet enough to learn or get our work done."
—"Everything would be a mess."
—"School wouldn't be any fun."

Distribute paper, and ask each student to list one or two rules that should be followed in the classroom. Explain that the group is going to create a "Classroom Constitution," a set of rules that will help make the classroom a safe, productive, enjoyable place for all. In your own words, elaborate:

Everyone will have an opportunity to contribute ideas for the rules and to vote on five or six rules for the class to agree upon and adopt. Keep in mind that everyone must be treated equally and fairly under the "Classroom Constitution."

When the students have finished their individual rule generation, divide the class into groups of three or four to share and discuss the importance of each person's rule suggestions. Explain that during the sharing it is okay for the students to think of another important rule or to change their minds about one or more of their original rules.

After the small groups have had time to process their rules, gather the whole class together and ask volunteers to state their rules while you write them on the board. List all stated rules, even those that are similar to ones already listed. Then discuss with the students which rules can be combined or which of two or more similar rules is easier to understand. Narrow the list down to rules that are distinctly different from one another. Make sure that as many decisions as possible are made by the group, but feel free to add any rule that you need. Tell the students: "I need to have this rule." Finally, have the students vote for the five most important rules they are willing to follow. Do this by a show of hands or by secret ballot.

List the rules on a large sheet of chart paper under the heading "Classroom Constitution." Under the rules write this statement: "I agree to follow these rules." Then ask the students to sign their names, thereby giving "public notice" of their agreement. Post the "Classroom Constitution" in a highly visible place in the room. In a follow-up discussion, extend thinking to more global issues.

Discussion Questions:
1. *How are laws made in our society?*
2. *Are we obligated to follow the laws of our country? Why?*
3. *Are all of our laws fair to every citizen? What do you think we can do to change unfair laws?*
4. *Why do we have penalties for people who break the law?*
5. *Do you think most people would follow society's laws even if there were no penalties? …Why or why not?*

Resolving Conflicts Fairly

Purpose:
To encourage moral thinking in problem-solving situations; to cultivate skills required to resolve conflicts fairly.

Materials:
chalkboard or whiteboard and writing implements; puppets (optional)

Procedure:
Prior to leading this activity, write down any conflicts observed in the classroom or on the playground. These conflicts may involve either your students or students from other classes.

Call a class meeting, and explain that you want to discuss a problem situation that you observed the day before. Write these headings across the top of the board: *Reasons, Feelings, Solutions*. Describe one of the conflicts that you observed. Instead of mentioning names, say "Person #1", "Person #2," etc., or use another way to identify the people involved without giving away their identities. Focus the students on the conflict and the moral issues, not on personalities.

Next, challenge the students to think of possible reasons for the problem. Invite them to discuss the reasons while you list them on the board under the first heading (Reasons). Then, ask the children to imagine how each of the parties in the conflict felt. As feeling words are shared, write them on the board under the second heading (Feelings).

Divide the class into groups of three or four and explain that their task is to brainstorm possible solutions to the conflict that are just and fair. Remind the students that seeking the advice of a responsible adult is an acceptable solution. Allow 5 to 10 minutes for brainstorming.

Ask the groups to choose their best solution and share it with the rest of the class. List alternative solutions on the board under the third heading (Solutions). Be sure to add any alternatives that you believe are important. When all alternatives are listed, discuss the probable consequences of each one. Then invite the students to select the best solution through a show-of-hands vote.

Finally, ask volunteers to role play the conflict, the feelings, and the identified solution. Following the role play, ask the actors and the audience:
—*Would this solution work in real life? ...Why or why not?*

If the students indicate that the solution is unworkable, discuss what is needed to make it work. Remind the students that some problems have no easy solutions and more than one alternative may have to be tested.

Extension:
Repeat this activity every day for a week to attune the students to resolving conflicts. After that, hold conflict-resolution meetings as the need arises. Conclude the activity with a summary discussion.

Discussion Questions:
1. *If you were involved in a similar conflict, how would you try to resolve it? Would your solution be fair to everyone involved?*
2. *Why is it important to think of different alternatives, rather than do the first thing that comes to mind?*
3. *How do you know if an alternative is just or unjust, fair or unfair?*
4. *What can you do if your solution to a problem doesn't work?*
5. *Why is it important to treat others fairly?*
6. *How can we let others know if they are treating us unfairly?*
7. *How can you stand up for yourself without causing a major conflict? What behaviors work best?*

What Is Prejudice?

Purpose:
To have students demonstrate understanding of the concept of prejudice and to discuss how prejudice hurts self and others.

Procedure:
Read the following story to the class:

> Once upon a time there was a boy named Tommy. Tommy was a nice boy who did well in school and had lots of friends. But Tommy had one peculiarity—he didn't like green peas. In fact, he really hated green peas. Although he had never eaten a green pea, he was sure if he did he would hate the taste. He wasn't exactly sure why he felt this way, he just knew that he did. Tommy wouldn't have anything to do with green peas; he just shut them out of his life and never had a good thing to say about them. As Tommy grew older his dislike for green peas grew and grew. One day he decided he didn't like green beans either, and then he didn't like lettuce. Pretty soon he disliked all green food, even pistachio ice cream! Since foods don't have any feelings, Tommy's negative attitude didn't hurt them. But Tommy sure missed out on a lot of good things!

After reading the story, write the word *prejudice* on the board and ask the students what the word means to them. Record all responses. As a class, select the most appropriate definition(s). Facilitate discussion by relating the prejudice (of Tommy in the story) toward green foods to prejudice toward people and groups of people.

Discussion Questions:
1. What was Tommy's reason for not liking green peas?
2. What do you think might happen if Tommy tried green peas and other green foods?
3. In what ways did Tommy miss out because of his prejudice against green foods?
4. How does ignorance (not getting to know someone or something) contribute to prejudice?
5. What are some ways that people show prejudice against others?
6. How do you think people feel when they experience prejudice from other people?

Extension:
Form small groups, and have each group create a role-play demonstrating one form of prejudice. Explain that the groups may either dramatize the effects of prejudice in real life or deal with fanciful themes, such as Tommy and the green peas. Have each group act out its play for the entire class.

Unit 5
Caring

Kind, compassionate, and generous behaviors arise from caring attitudes that cannot simply be "taught." Children learn to care for others first by being cared for themselves. They also learn to care by accepting custodial and nurturing responsibilities, such as for pets, and by helping others and being positively reinforced for their efforts.

One of the most effective ways for students to learn the value of caring is through participation in formal service programs and projects. An entire class might assume responsibility for making regular visits to a retirement home, doing chores and errands for elderly individuals living near the school, providing a graffiti watch and removal service, or collecting blankets and food for citizens who are homeless.

To derive maximum learning from service projects, treat them as you would any other subject. Prepare students by teaching them the requisite skills, supervise their efforts, provide ongoing motivation and further training, and give them regular opportunities to discuss and write about their experiences.

Additional ways to promote caring attitudes and actions:

- Be a caregiver to your students. Treat them with love and respect, carefully guiding their interactions, reinforcing pro-social behavior, and helping them to resolve conflicts.

- Facilitate students getting to know each other. Encourage them to accept and respect individual differences, to include everyone as an important member of the group, to be sensitive to each other's feelings, to cooperate and collaborate.

- Teach a conflict resolution process and insist that students use it to find peaceful, win-win solutions to interpersonal problems.

- Talk to the students about specific community service projects in which you are involved.
- Always show consideration for others — parents, other teachers, school staff, counselors, and administrators.
- Demonstrate your willingness to go the extra mile for any student who is struggling.

Real People Who Care

Purpose:
By reciting and dramatizing a story about a caring individual, students identify, experience, and discuss a variety of caring behaviors. They further explore the concept of caring by examining historical figures and events.

Materials:
copies of the experience sheet, *Albert Schweitzer, Reverence for Life*, for each student

Procedure:
Pass out the experience sheet on Albert Schweitzer. Either read to or have the students read the story. After the story, identify and discuss the caring behaviors of Albert Schweitzer.

After the discussion, ask volunteers to dramatize the key events in the story. Review the story sequence and allow the students to improvise the dialogue. After the first dramatization, ask a new group of volunteers to dramatize the same story. After a rehearsal, have the groups take turns dramatizing their story in front of the class. Then lead the class in a discussion of the events and character motivations.

When the dramatizations have been completed, extend the concept of caring to other historical figures and events. Talk about other people who performed caring and courageous deeds. Some examples are:
- Harriet Tubman, who risked her life many times to help her people escape slavery.
- Sequoya, the Cherokee Indian who worked for 12 years to create an alphabet of 86 signs to put the Cherokee language into writing.
- Florence Nightengale, who nursed many people back to health.
- John Muir, who helped to preserve the natural beauty of the land by collaborating in the creation of the National Parks.
- Dr. Martin Luther King, Jr., who lost his life working for the equal rights of all people.
- Peter Zenger, a colonial newspaperman who dared to print the truth about the wrongdoings of a public figure.

Ask the students to share about people they know who have performed caring deeds. Summarize the activity be asking some thought-provoking questions and facilitating discussion.

Discussion Questions:
1. *Why do people dedicate or risk their lives for the sake of others?*
2. *How can you show that you care at home? ...at school? ...in the neighborhood?*
3. *When we care about someone or something, what are the feelings that we typically experience?*
4. *How do we benefit by caring about an issue? ...an event? ...an individual or group of people?*

Adaptations:
Rather than just discussing historical figures, have the students choose a figure they would like to research. As a summary to their research, have the students write a story about their character and read it to the class.

Albert Schweitzer
Reverence for Life

The dark waters of the river held many unseen terrors, but Albert Schweitzer was not afraid as he returned to his hospital in deepest Africa. He had travelled this river many times, and he knew that if he and his guide respected the animals and rowed peacefully through the waters, they would be in no danger.

Dr. Schweitzer was anxious to get back to his hospital even though he often had to work in terrible conditions. The hospital was far from civilization, and because it was near the equator, it had one of the worst climates on earth. It was hot and humid all the time and torrential rains could bring flood waters. There were also creepy, crawly bugs, stinging spiders, annoying mosquitoes, deadly snakes, and big gorillas. When Dr. Schweitzer first started his hospital he didn't have much money, but he knew he had to begin somewhere so his first hospital building had been an old chicken coup that he worked very hard to make into a building that could serve people as a hospital.

As a young boy in the quiet villages of the Vosqes Mountains of Germany (later France), Albert led a rather unremarkable childhood. He was shy, not particularly a good student, and considered a day dreamer. In those early years there was no sign of the important work he would do later in his life. He did, however, always have a passion for reading which he kept his entire life. He said that if he started a book he wouldn't put it down until finished, and if he enjoyed a book he would read it two or three times. Perhaps it was this interest in reading that turned him into a very curious teenager who wanted to know the answers to everything. He was so inquisitive that he would often make an annoying nuisance of himself.

As a young adult in his twenties, Albert's many interests developed into a variety of activities and work. He wrote books, he became a church pastor, the principal of a seminary, and a university professor. He also began a life-long musical career as an organist. He travelled to many countries giving concerts from which he earned enough money for his education and later for his African hospital.

Even with all his success, Albert Schweitzer was not satisfied. At the age of 30, he became aware of the great need Africans had for medical care and decided to become a medical doctor and devote his life to healing the people of Africa. Many of his friends tried to convince him not to go to Africa. He was a success in Europe, they reminded him, and Africa was a strange and scary place. His friends told him there were witch doctors and cannibals and terrible diseases there. But suffering of any kind upset Albert, and he wanted to make a difference whether it was with a helpless animal or the natives of Africa. Albert knew he had to do something. He wrote to his friends, "I could not just be talking about caring for others. My medicine is putting into practice the love I feel for all living things."

It was this belief that led him to hit upon the phrase, "Reverence for life." These simple words came to represent for him the meaning and purpose of his whole existence. At age 37, Albert Schweitzer opened his hospital and the direction of the rest of his life was set. At first, his little hospital in the jungle had no electricity, only simple grass mattresses on the floor, and the roof leaked whenever it rained. But he knew what medicine and kind words the people needed to heal. Little by little his hospital grew as did his reputation.

Over the years, more people came to work with him and the hospital never stopped growing. With his own money he earned from book royalties, concerts, and speaking engagements, and the donations from all over the world he expanded the hospital to over 70 buildings and over 600 beds for its patients. Schweitzer also continued to receive many awards and recognition for his work. In 1952, at the age of 78, he was awarded the Noble Peace Prize, one of the highest honors anyone can receive. Along with the peace prize he also received $30,000. As could be expected of Albert Schweitzer, he didn't use any of the money for himself, but instead, used the money to add another building to his hospital. Such was his dedication and "reverence for life."

Dr. Albert Schweitzer

A Caring Project

Purpose:
This activity raises student awareness of caring feelings and caretaking actions by giving students an opportunity to practice concrete caring behaviors on a daily basis.

Materials:
writing paper or composition books; writing implements; copies of the three *My Caring Project* experience sheets for each student

Procedure:
Introduce this activity by asking the students, "What do you care about?" Discuss various things for which the students experience feelings of caring and concern, such as getting good grades, the well-being of family members, having friends, or learning how to read better. Discuss, too, any real threats that cause concern, such as floods, neighborhood crime, or earthquakes. Next, ask the students, "What do you *take care of* on a regular basis?" If the students have difficulty answering, offer suggestions, e.g., pet, plant, younger sibling.

In your own words, explain the assignment:

Everyone is going to choose a "caring project," which will involve taking care of something for the next two weeks. You will keep a log, writing down the things you do and how you feel about your project. The purpose of the project is to help you become more aware of the importance of caring for things.

Think of something that you can take care of for the next two weeks. It can be a pet that you already have, a plant, some aspect of the environment, or an object such as a bike. You might want to agree to take care of a brother or sister for a certain amount of time each day. Perhaps you'd like to volunteer to take a neighbor's dog for a walk every day. If you choose an object, like a bike, you must do something every day to take care of it. For example, you can wipe it clean, wash it, polish it, oil it, tighten the screws, put air in the tires, and put it in a place out of the weather. If you choose the environment, you can do things like pick up trash from the sidewalks, reuse paper that has writing only on one side, recycle cans or newspapers, or turn off unneeded lights at home. You will have one day to decide on a project and to get permission from a parent or other adult, if necessary.

Give the students their copies of the experiences sheets. Ask the students to fill in the top part of the experience sheet with their names, what or who they will take care of, and their list of specific activities.

Next, instruct the students to write down exactly what they do each day, as well as how they feel about it. Tell them: *Something must be recorded after each date, even if you forget to keep your agreement. Should this happen, explain why you did not complete a caring action and how you feel about having forgotten.*

If you like, keep the logs at school, and allow time each morning for the students to record their activities from the previous day.

At the end of the project, invite the students to share their entries with the class. Conclude the activity with a wrap-up discussion.

Discussion Questions:
1. How did you feel when you kept your agreement and followed through? If you forgot, how did you feel about that?
2. What effect did writing about your project daily have on your actions? Was your caretaking better or worse? Why?
3. Why is it important to care for (and take care of) people, places, animals, and things?
4. Do we care more about people and things when we take care of them? Why or why not?

EXPERIENCE SHEET

My Caring Project

For the next two weeks, I _____ agree to take
Name

care of _____.

I will do this by _____

_____

_____

Day 1

What I did _____   How I felt about what I did _____

_____   _____

_____   _____

Day 2

What I did _____   How I felt about what I did _____

_____   _____

_____   _____

Day 3

What I did _____   How I felt about what I did _____

_____   _____

_____   _____

Day 4

What I did _____   How I felt about what I did _____

_____   _____

_____   _____

EXPERIENCE SHEET

Day 5

What I did _____   How I felt about what I did _____

_____   _____

_____   _____

Day 6

What I did _____   How I felt about what I did _____

_____   _____

_____   _____

Day 7

What I did _____   How I felt about what I did _____

_____   _____

_____   _____

Day 8

What I did _____   How I felt about what I did _____

_____   _____

_____   _____

Day 9

What I did _____   How I felt about what I did _____

_____   _____

_____   _____

EXPERIENCE SHEET

Day 10

What I did _____   How I felt about what I did _____

_____   _____

_____   _____

Day 11

What I did _____   How I felt about what I did _____

_____   _____

_____   _____

Day 12

What I did _____   How I felt about what I did _____

_____   _____

_____   _____

Day 13

What I did _____   How I felt about what I did _____

_____   _____

_____   _____

Day 14

What I did _____   How I felt about what I did _____

_____   _____

_____   _____

Friendship Profile

Purpose:
To identify the characteristics of a friend or caring person.

Materials:
writing paper, pencils, butcher paper, colored markers, and scissors

Procedure:
Introduce this activity by setting a mood in which the students can think about what characterizes a friend. Read a poem or story about friendship, such as "Androcles and the Lion," a fable by Aesop, or ask the students to respond to a quote like, "A True Friend Is the Best Possession," by Benjamin Franklin. You might sing the well-known song, "It's a Small World," made famous at Disneyland, which speaks about world-wide friendships and the common language of smiles, which mean friendship to everyone.

After the warm-up activity, ask the students to begin thinking about what they look for in a friend.

Next, have the students form groups of four to six. Explain the task:

Your job is to come up with ideas about what makes a friend. As you discuss the characteristics of a friend, list words that describe what a friend is like and things that a friend does — a friend's actions or behaviors. Choose one person in your group to record the ideas on a piece of writing paper.

If groups have difficulty getting started, make a few suggestions to trigger ideas. Words and phrases might include: *helpful, cooperative, caring, working together, generous, sharing, thoughtful, polite, courteous, kind, loving, sympathetic, compassionate, nice, smiles at me, spends time with me*, and *listens to me*.

When the groups have finished their lists, give each group several colored markers and a piece of butcher paper on which to trace the body of one group member. Have each group select one member to lie down on the paper, and another to trace around the body with a pencil. Have a third group member refine the penciled outline by tracing over it with a colored marker. Have still another member cut out the paper body. Instruct the groups to copy the ideas they listed during discussion onto their body outline with colored markers. Encourage everyone to take a turn recording several words or phrases. Suggest that the students write large and try to fill the whole body with the characteristics of a friend.

Invite each group to share its completed profile with the class. Post the paper bodies around the classroom or on a bulletin board titled, "What Is a Friend?" Debrief the activity with a discussion.

Discussion Questions:
1. *How might your life be different if you had all the traits that make up a good friend?*
2. *How would the world change if everyone demonstrated the characteristics of a friend?*
3. *What is one characteristic that you would like to acquire? What will you do to acquire it?*

Adaptation:
When using this activity with upper graders, consider substituting the words "caring person" for "friend." The objective is for students to become caring toward others in general, even those who are not personal friends. Upper graders do not relate to all classmates as friends.

Giving and Receiving Praise

Purpose:
To encourage students to recognize each other's positive attributes and to acknowledge those attributes in writing.

Materials:
small squares of writing paper; pencils; paper lunch bags; crayons or colored markers

Procedure:
Begin this activity by asking the students how they feel when another person compliments them or acknowledges them for doing something well. Ask volunteers to share their feelings. Explain that all people need and want to hear positive things about themselves. Hearing praise from others makes people want to keep doing the things for which other people are praising them. Tell the students that they can encourage and support each other by exchanging positive words of praise on a regular basis.

Tell the students that they are going to have an opportunity to practice giving each other positive acknowledgments so that this behavior can become habitual.

Give each student a paper lunch bag and some crayons or colored markers. Ask each person to print his/her name on the bag in large letters and decorate the bag with crayons or markers. Suggest that the students draw designs, symbols, or pictures that represent something about themselves.

When the bags are decorated, give each student a stack of writing paper equivalent in amount to the number of students in the class. Give the following instructions:

Pass your bag to the person on your right (in front, in back, etc.). When you receive a bag, look at the name on the bag, take the first piece of paper from your stack, and write a note of praise to that person. The note should contain some positive words about the person or his/her accomplishments. No put downs or criticisms are allowed. You do not have to sign your name to the note. When you are finished writing the note, put it in the bag and pass it to the next person. Keep passing the bags until you receive your own bag back, full of positive notes.

Set aside time for the students to read the notes they receive. Invite students to share their most meaningful notes of praise and tell why those notes are especially positive, encouraging, and/or supportive. Ask students to share how they feel about receiving acknowledgments from their peers. Conclude by discussing the importance of verbally acknowledging others and sharing feelings of appreciation.

Discussion Questions:
1. *Why is it important for us to acknowledge each other with positive words?*
2. *How can we let people know that we appreciate their caring actions?*
3. *How would our lives be different if we supported each other daily with words of praise and acknowledgment?*
4. *What must you do in order to have something positive to say to each person in class? (Get to know the person; notice what the person does.)*
5. *How do we learn to be caring people?*

Adaptations:
This activity can be adapted in several ways to suit the ability and maturity of your class. For example, have your students focus on just one person per day. Or lead the entire class through a sequence of note-writing, with everyone addressing to the same person at the same time. Collect each set of notes and "screen out" negative or questionable notes before giving the remainder to the intended recipient.

Caring Is the Big Story

Purpose:
To highlight and acknowledge the good works of others.

Materials:
newspapers, news magazines; videos of television newscasts (optional); writing materials

Procedure:
Share a newspaper account about a person who did something good. Explain that much of what we read in the newspapers or see on television newscasts is negative. We see people breaking the law or doing things to hurt other people. Emphasize that many people do good things that help other people. Refer to the example in your news article or tell about events you know of in which people have performed helpful and caring deeds. Cite examples of people who have helped others in natural disasters such as earthquakes, floods, and hurricanes. Tell about people who have made breakthroughs in the medical field or invented things that helped humanity.

Ask the students to look through newspapers and/or news magazines and cut out articles that feature people who have performed good deeds. Invite the students to look at television newscasts over the next few days and write their own accounts of good works in action. As an alternative, have the students write about caring actions they have seen in the classroom or throughout the school. After the students share their news stories, post the stories on a bulletin board under the heading, "Who Cares in the News?"

After a variety of news stories have been collected and shared, ask the students to choose one person (or group) who performed a caring act and write letters to that person. Invite the students to praise the person for his/her actions and thank the person for contributing to the world, the nation, the community, the school, or the classroom. Address the letters to the individual in care of the newspaper or magazine in which the article was published or the television station from which the news was broadcast.

Conclude the activity with a summary discussion.

Discussion Questions:
1. Why is it important to thank people who perform caring acts?
2. How would the school, community, nation, or world be different if we all did good deeds every day?
3. What would the world be like if no one made the effort to perform good deeds?

The Kindness Book

Purpose:
The students will brainstorm examples of kind deeds and then describe a kind act they did or received.

Materials:
writing materials; drawing paper; colored marking pens, crayons, or pencils; glue; a large three-ring binder

Procedure:
Write the word *kindness* on the board. Ask the students to help you define its meaning. In the process, make these points about kindness:
- Kindness is a quality that is developed from being kind.
- Being kind means being considerate, thoughtful, or helpful.
- An act of kindness is something you *do*. It is a deed or behavior. It's possible to have kind thoughts and feelings, but they are private until you *express* them in an act of kindness.
- A kind act is always done voluntarily, not because it is required.

Ask the students to brainstorm examples of kind acts. List their suggestions on the board. Encourage a variety of ideas, by asking questions like "What are some kind acts you can do for a friend? ...classmate? ...brother or sister? ...parent? ...neighbor? ...your teacher? ...grandparent? ...a stranger? ...the environment? Include things like:
—make friends with a new student
—offer to share things
—talk to or play with kids who seem left out
—give someone a compliment
—read a story to a younger child
—visit senior citizens in a retirement or rest home
—help a friend do his/her chores
—help a classmate solve a tough math problem
—surprise your parent by doing an "extra" chore at home
—hold a door for someone
—pick up trash when you see it lying around

Announce that the students are going to write about and/or draw an act of kindness they've done — or one that someone else has done for them. Distribute writing and drawing materials. In your own words, explain:

Describe the kind act, tell who did it, and for whom it was done. You don't have to mention names, just use words like "friend," "teacher," "sister," or "older person." Then write about the feelings of the person who did the kind deed, and the feelings of the person who received it. Draw a picture that shows the kind act being done.

Use whatever system you normally use to have the students correct their spelling and grammar and then complete a rewrite. As a final step, have the students assemble the story and drawing, either by writing a final version somewhere on the drawing itself, or by gluing the drawing to the story page, or vice-versa.

Have the students share their stories and pictures in small groups. Then place all of the finished work in the three-ring binder. Insert a cover page titled, "Book of Kindness." (Have one of the children illustrate the cover page.)

Note:
Adjust the demands of the assignment to the ability levels of your students. Younger students need only write a paragraph or two; older ones could be asked to write a true or fictional story about kindness.

Discussion Questions:
1. Why is it important to try to turn kind thoughts into kind deeds?
2. When you have a kind thought about someone, how can you express it?
3. Why can't chores and assignments ever be acts of kindness?
4. Why do acts of kindness have to be voluntary?

Caring and Kindness in the News

Purpose:
To identify acts of caring and kindness and to be able to relate kind and caring actions to civic duty and responsibility.

Materials:
examples of one or two acts of kindness in stories or photos clipped from newspapers; copies of local newspapers, organizational newsletters, and other publications that carry human-interest stories; construction paper; glue; dark-colored marking pens

Note:
The research portion of this activity can be given as homework or as a library assignment, with the students assuming responsibility for finding appropriate publications.

Procedure:
Review with the students the definition of an act of kindness:
—considerate, thoughtful, or helpful
—an action, not merely a thought
—voluntary

Read the examples of kind and caring acts that you have clipped from the newspaper. (Or show them if they are photos.)

Tell the students that you want them to become aware of the kind things that people do for one another, and that one way to do this is to start noticing reports of kind deeds in newspapers and other publications.

Point out that news-reporting organizations, including TV, radio, and newspapers, don't devote very much time or space to reporting "good" news, including good deeds, because such things are not usually considered "news." However, examples of kind acts *can* be found. For example, a report of hurricane damage might tell about people who have donated blankets and clothing to help the victims. A story about an accident might include a photo of a child being comforted. In addition, most newspapers report on voluntary community activities, like clean-ups, food drives, or other benefits. All of these examples fit the kindness definition.

Tell the students that you want them to search through newspapers and other types of publications to find examples of kind acts. If you are providing the publications, distribute them. If the students are responsible, describe the procedure.

When the students have collected their articles, distribute the construction paper, glue, and markers.

Have the students mount their article on a sheet of construction paper slightly larger than the article itself. Using the marking pen, have them circle or underline the part that describes the deed. Then have them write a new headline for the article that focuses on the act of kindness. For example, if the article was titled, "Hurricane Rosie Batters Florida Coast," the new headline might read, "Thousands Send Aid to Florida."

Have the students get together in groups of four to six and share their articles. Then post the articles on a bulletin board, under the caption "Caring and Kindness Makes News!"

Discussion Questions:
1. *How did the act of kindness you found out about help the person(s) who received it?*
2. *Why is it important not to ignore acts of kindness or take them for granted?*
3. *Why do people help each other in time of need?*
4. *How do you feel when you do something kind for another person?*

The Link of Kindness

Purpose:
The students will do kind things for one another and thereby develop an understanding that acts of kindness are self-perpetuating because they promote a spirit of giving and generosity.

Materials:
strips of colored construction paper or other sturdy art paper; marking pens, stapler or tape; box or basket for collecting finished links; a dinner bell or chime

Procedure:
Announce that the class is going to create a "Chain of Kindness" that reaches all around the room. Explain that the chain will be very colorful and attractive and that everyone will have an opportunity to participate in its making. However, the speed with which the chain reaches around the room will depend on how many acts of kindness the students do for each other.

Hold up one of the paper strips. Explain that each link in the chain will be made from a strip just like this one, and show the students where the strips will be kept. (Place the blank strips, markers, and box/basket together, perhaps at an activity center bearing the name *Kindness*.) Then make the first link as a demonstration. Tell the students about a kind act that you did for someone in the class that day (or describe a kind act that you observed a student do). Then, using a dark marker, write a sentence describing the kind action on the strip. Loop and staple the strip to make a link, with the writing on the outside. Tape the first link to a secure location, such as the frame of a bulletin board.

In your own words explain:

Each of you can make and add links to the chain by doing acts of kindness for members of the class. Remember an act of kindness must be a helpful, considerate or thoughtful <u>action</u>. It must also be voluntary — something you do because you want to, not because you have to. When you do a kind act, get a strip of paper and write a sentence on it describing what you did. You may also make a strip for someone who is kind to you as long as that person doesn't make one, too. Only one strip per kind action. Put your finished strip in the box/basket. Once a day, we'll read all the links. If your description fits the definition of an act of kindness, you'll get to attach your link to the chain. There is no limit to the number of links you can add — as long as each one is for a different act of kindness.

Once a day, read aloud the completed strips from the box/basket. After a strip is read, allow the student who did the kindness to attach and staple the strip to the end of the chain, making a new link. If you have a bell or chime, ring it while you announce the addition of a new link to the kindness chain.

Discussion Questions:
1. When someone is kind to you, are you more likely or less likely to be kind to others? Why?
2. Is kindness "catching?" How is it spread?
3. How do you feel when someone does something kind for you?
4. How do you feel when you know you've made someone feel good?
5. What are some examples of very small acts of kindness? What are some examples of very big acts of kindness?
6. If everyone in our class tried to make one extra person feel good each day, how would our class benefit?

Unit 6
Citizenship

Children can learn the value of citizenship by experiencing the impact of their individual efforts in the close knit community of the classroom and in the larger school community. They can learn that they do make a difference when they follow a rule, voice their opinion, vote, properly dispose of trash, work and play cooperatively with other students, listen and stay informed, do their part to make special events successful, respect authority, perform voluntary school service, and keep their parents involved by taking home notices and inviting participation.

When meaningful civic values help define a child's relationship to his/her immediate environment, those values can logically and developmentally be extended to the community, the nation, and the world.

Methods of fostering good citizenship include:

- Teach civic values through academic subjects, the news, TV, and literature. Examine the actions of real people and give them citizenship "grades."

- Find ways of connecting civic values to home and community.

- Display photos and portraits of noteworthy citizens, as well as posters and quotations that reflect the virtues of good citizenship.

- Teach a process for democratic problem solving that includes consideration for all points of view, discussion, debate, and consensus seeking or voting.

- Involve students in decision making and encourage them to share responsibility for making the classroom a positive place to learn.

- Hold regular class meetings to discuss issues and problems that arise, such as disruptive behavior, stealing, social cliques, and hurtful language.

- Involve the students in the creation and enforcement of rules, and in decisions regarding the consequences of breaking rules.

- Talk about how you work with other teachers, counselors, administrators, parents, and board members to determine the policies of the school and illustrate for students how their needs, wishes, and requests impact the governing of the school.

- During election campaigns, talk with your students about voting. Show voter registration cards and sample ballots. When elections are over, explain who won and by how many votes. Cover local as well as national elections, helping students to recognize that individual votes make a difference.

The Rules of the Game

Purpose:
To create a game using miscellaneous materials and teach it to the class; to describe the rules of the game in writing; to explain how rules and laws help people live and work together effectively.

Materials:
four to six boxes, each containing several small objects, (whistles, balls, sticks, shoes, tools, etc.); writing materials

Procedure:
Introduce the activity by asking the students to think of some games that they like to play. Pick two or three games and talk about those games in some depth. Choose athletic games that are played one-to-one (tennis, badminton) or in teams (softball, soccer, basketball), board games (chess, Monopoly), and other indoor games (Scrabble, Trivial Pursuits). Discuss how the games are played, focusing in particular on rules. Make the following points, jotting notes on the board:

- Rules ensure an even start, safety, and adherence to certain agreed-upon behaviors throughout the game.
- Rules protect both the players and the object of the game.
- To play any game well, you have to know the rules, play as skillfully as you can, and respect the rights of your opponent.
- In some games, points are lost by making fouls. Too many fouls can disqualify a player from the game.
- Fouls occur when you break the rules of the game, either accidentally or intentionally.
- Fouls are behaviors that are not allowed because they create an unfair advantage, are disrespectful or dangerous, or destroy the object of the game.

Divide the students into groups of four to six. Distribute the boxes of objects and writing materials. Then explain:

Look at the objects in your box. Your task is to create a game using some or all of those objects. Decide what rules are necessary in order for the game to work. How are points won and lost? Do fouls occur when certain rules are broken? What is the penalty for breaking a rule? Give your game a name, and have a scribe write down the rules. Be prepared to teach the game to the rest of the class, explaining the rules that govern it.

Circulate while the students are working. Offer ideas and suggestions as needed.

Have the groups take turns teaching their games and rules to the rest of the class. If possible, play each game for a short period of time. (You may need to spread this portion of the activity over several days.)

After each game, lead a short discussion. As you debrief the game, develop an analogy between playing successfully (by the rules) and living life successfully, as a law-abiding citizen.

Discussion Questions:
1. Would any other rules help make this game more fun?
2. Were any of the rules unnecessary?
3. Should any of the rules be changed?
4. Why do we need rules?
5. How are the rules that must be followed in a game similar to the rules that must be followed at school? How are they similar to the laws of the community? ...the nation?
6. What would happen if we didn't have rules and laws?
7. Who makes rules at school? ...at home?
8. Who makes the laws of our community? ...our nation?
9. Are all rules and laws good? How can we tell when a rule or law isn't fair or isn't working well?
10. When laws are unjust or don't work well, can they be challenged or changed? How?

The Trial

Purpose:
By interviewing adults and sharing insights gained from these interviews, the students develop awareness of how this nation's justice system works.

Materials:
writing materials

Procedure:
Intrigue the children by telling them about a trial you were involved in as a juror, witness, or observer. (The best example will be one that is not complex, but straightforward, and does not involve a heinous crime.) Tell the students about the proceedings, verdict, and whether or not the verdict was just in your opinion. Then ask:

Have you ever watched a real trial or a television program about a trial? If so, you know how interesting trials can be. The jury and the judge try to do the right thing, but it isn't always easy.

Announce that the students are going to have a chance to interview an adult who participated in a trial as a juror, witness or observer. Explain that their task is to find out what happened during the trial. Afterwards, they will share what they learned in small groups. Reassure the students that they will probably not have to look far to find a person to interview. Suggest that they check with family members, neighbors, and friends first, and, if necessary, request that those people ask co-workers and other acquaintances.

Provide time parameters. Then ask the students to help you brainstorm questions to ask the interviewees. After brainstorming, involve the students in evaluating the questions, choosing the best ones, and putting them in a logical order. Have the students copy the list. Here is a sample:

Interview Questions

1. What was the court case about?

2. Was there a jury?

3. If the case involved a jury, who was on trial and what were the charges?

4. If there was no jury, who were the opposing parties and what were they claiming?

5. What did the witnesses say?

6. What was the outcome?

7. Do you think the outcome was just?

When the students have completed their interviews, direct them to meet in triads and share their findings. Give each child 3 minutes to describe and summarize the trial to the other two triad members. Call time after each 3-minute interval.

Finally, conduct a "listening check." Have each triad member take 1 minute to verbally summarize (reflect) the report of one other person in the triad. Conclude with a class discussion.

Discussion Questions:
1. *Why do people serve as witnesses and jurors in court cases?*
2. *What are the judge's responsibilities during a trial?*
3. *Why are opposing parties usually represented by lawyers? What are the responsibilities of lawyers?*
4. *What kind of agreement does a jury have to come to? (unanimous agreement) Why?*

Speak Up for What You Believe In

Purpose:
By researching and reporting on the lives of famous and ordinary people who stood up for what they believed was right or pursued a seemingly impossible goal, the students gain insight into the courage required to make a public stand.

Materials:
the names of famous and ordinary people, and groups written on self-stick labels and placed in a container (suggestions below); writing materials; costumes and props (optional)

Procedure:
Prior to leading this activity, prepare a collection of identification labels and place them in a container. Choose from the following suggestions and/or select the names of individuals and groups relevant to a current (or recent) unit of study.

Based on the number of students group, prepare the labels so that when they are all drawn the students will be divided into teams of three or four. Each team will be working on one individual, group, or issue.

Famous Individuals:
George Washington
Thomas Jefferson
Abraham Lincoln
Harriet Tubman
Carrie Nation
Susan B. Anthony
Franklin D. Roosevelt
Eleanor Roosevelt
Mahatma Gandhi
Martin Luther King Jr.
Cesar Chavez
Jesse Jackson
Bella Abzug
Mikhail Gorbachev
Nelson Mandela

Issues Debated by Ordinary Citizens and Groups:
- English rule prior to the American Revolution
- Treatment of Indians and slaves
- Women not being allowed to vote
- Annihilation of the buffalo
- Child labor
- Railroads built across the lands of Indians and farmers
- Factory owners recruiting immigrants with false promises
- The fairness of the idea, "separate, but equal"
- Treatment of laborers prior to the formation of unions
- The injustice of Japanese internment camps during W.W.II

Groups Acting for a Cause
(3 or 4 labels for each):
- Participants in the "Boston Tea Party"
- Soldiers in America's wars
- Freedom Riders
- Modern environmentalists

Show the students the container of labels and explain the assignment:

You will have a chance to draw a label from this container. Some of the people whose names are on the labels are famous and some are not. Some labels list issues that ordinary citizens debated openly and courageously, sometimes for many years. Other labels list groups that came together to act for a specific cause.. If you draw this last type of label, take a few moments to locate the other members of your group before beginning work.

Your task is to give a presentation on the individual whose name (group, or issue description) you draw. Do research and gather as much information as you need to represent your character, group, or issue well. Be creative in your presentation. You can create a dance, or song, or artwork, or anything that you think will inform the rest of the class.

When you make your presentation, tell the class who you are and when you lived (if you are no longer living), and give us enough background information to understand your presentation.

Have the students draw labels and form teams with the other students who drew the same labels. Provide time for research as well as group planning sessions. Assist, as necessary. Let the students know when their presentations will be made in class.

Facilitate the presentations, ensuring audience understanding by asking questions about context, date, history, etc. Applaud each presentation and urge the class to ask questions of the presenters. Conclude the activity with a summary discussion.

Discussion Questions:
1. *How are our lives today affected by what these people said and did?*
2. *Many of these individuals were shunned and degraded, even badly hurt, for taking a stand in public. Why do people risk their safety to speak out?*
3. *How can we show that we appreciate the good things that have come from what some of these people did?*
4. *What are some current issues that are causing people to speak out?*

A Classroom Campaign

Purpose:
By investigating the issues surrounding a current or recent political race or ballot proposition and conducting a classroom campaign, the students discover how candidates and issues capture the attention and motivation of voters.

Note: The next activity, "Debates and Voting," is an excellent follow-up to this activity.

Materials:
information relevant to a ballot proposition or elected office, including statements in sample ballots, articles, and advertisements; art materials for posters, placards, etc.

Procedure:
Announce to the students that they are going to do some campaigning. Guide them in selecting a clear cut, well-publicized current or recent political race or state/local proposition. If any students have strong opinions about the chosen race, allow those students to form a team representing their side; then divide the remaining students between the two teams — one team favoring each candidate or each side of the selected issue. You should end up with two groups of approximately equal size. In your own words, point out:

As this campaign develops, keep an open mind and listen to both sides carefully. Even those of you who feel certain which side you are on now might change your mind at some point. Just listen to the information that the campaign reveals and decide for yourself what (or who) is best.

Provide information (statements in sample ballots, articles, advertisements, etc.) to both groups, and allow them to "caucus" and plan their campaigns. Schedule class time for preparation, demonstrations, and presentations. Provide art materials to students who wish to make posters, placards, hats, and other items for their campaign.

Facilitate campaign demonstrations and presentations in which both groups create excitement and promote their point of view. Encourage the groups to reveal the issues that are most important to their side. After the last campaign event, have the students vote on the issue, or for the candidate of their choice (or conduct the next activity, "How to Make Your Opinion Count!", which includes voting). Tally the votes and announce the winner. If possible, compare classroom results with the actual election outcome. Lead a summary discussion.

Discussion Questions:
1. *What did you learn by participating in this campaign?*
2. *What are the purposes of campaigning?*
3. *Why is it important for citizens to exercise their right to vote?*
4. *Many adults who are registered to vote, don't vote. Sometimes as many as half fail to go to the polls. Why do you think that is?*

Variation:
Don't wait for election season to conduct this activity. Look at important issues currently being debated before the U.S. Congress, state legislature, or local governing body (city council, county board of supervisors, etc.). Parallel actual events with classroom debates, negotiations, and voting. Have the students compare their results with actual outcomes. Have older students examine media analyses of resulting laws/decisions and their anticipated impact.

Debates and Voting

Purpose:
By conducting debates followed by a secret-ballot vote on a specific elected office or political issue, the students experience how elections are won and lost.

Note: The previous activity, "A Classroom Campaign" is an excellent lead-in to this activity.

Materials:
two podiums for debaters; table and chairs for moderators; ballots and a ballot box

Procedure:
If your class did not complete, "A Classroom Campaign" (previous activity), before proceeding select a recent or current ballot proposition or political race and divide the class into two opposing groups, one representing each side.

Begin by asking the students: *Have you ever listened to a real debate between candidates for an elected office or proponents of opposing sides of a ballot proposition?*

Have each team choose three spokespersons to take turns speaking on behalf of the team's preferred candidate or side of the ballot issue (for or against). Explain that each debater will respond to two questions in front of the class, and that the teams will have a chance to prepare the debaters by brainstorming ideas for their arguments and coaching them to express themselves well.

Have each team develop six questions to ask the debaters (one question per debater). This means that three questions will be posed to members of their own team, who can be coached in advance to answer those questions in certain ways. The other three questions will be asked members of the opposing team, who will have no advance knowledge of the questions.

Announce that, after the debates, the students will hold a classroom election and vote on the candidates or issue. Instruct the students to listen carefully and make up their own minds about how to vote. Urge them to be open to new ideas and information, and to vote as individuals, regardless of which team they are on during the debates.

Place two podiums at the front of the classroom. Place the commentators' table and six chairs in front of and facing the podiums. Guide the debate process, as follows: Two debaters (one from each team) face the commentators. Two commentators (one per team) each direct one question to both debaters, who take turns responding. Next, two new debaters come to the podiums and respond to two new questions from two new commentators. Finally, the last two debaters come to the podiums and respond to the last two questions from the last two commentators.

Following the debates, distribute the ballots and allow the students to mark them and place them in the ballot box. Select an ad-hoc committee with members from both sides to count the ballots under your supervision and announce the outcome.

Bring out the refreshments and allow the students to enjoy a celebration. Encourage impromptu speeches by members of both teams. Winners may revel in their victory and reach out to the losers. Encourage members of the losing team to show good sportsmanship by pledging to support the choice of the majority. Conclude the activity with a brief discussion.

Discussion Questions:
1. *Why have a debate before an election?*
2. *Why is it important for eligible voters to vote?*
3. *When you are old enough to vote, what will you do to inform yourself about the candidates and issues?*
4. *What would it be like to live in a country where voting was not allowed?*

Unit 7
Reflections

Moral reflection helps students develop the ability to make moral judgments about their own behavior and that of others. As follow-up to the sections dealing with specific moral values, the activities in this unit offer students repeated opportunities to:

1. See the moral dimensions in everyday life situations.
2. Demonstrate understanding of the moral values presented in this book.
3. Practice taking the perspective of others.
4. Exercise their ability to reason morally.
5. Make thoughtful, moral decisions concerning typical life situations.
6. Gain self-knowledge by reflecting on their own actions in morally challenging situations.

Throughout these summary activities students are asked to identify the moral values operating in each situation. Permanently displaying a list of the six moral values presented in this book and their definitions will facilitate this process.

Ask the students what universal moral values they can identify as playing a role in each story or incident described. Help them identify specific behaviors on the part of the people involved that are right, as well as specific behaviors that violate a universal moral value and are, therefore, wrong.

Encourage students to express their feelings about individual and fictional characters — what they admire, dislike, fear, or would like to emulate.

Stop the reading or action (in the case of role plays) at critical points and ask the students what would be the right thing to do in the situation at that moment. Or ask them to identify what is actually going on in the situation — who is doing what to whom and why.

In making decisions about what to do in a situation, insist that the students rely less on gut feelings and more on available information and evidence. Help them evaluate and apply the evidence.

Lead the students in brainstorming alternative actions and solutions. Evaluate each alternative and select one that is both morally sound and effective.

When appropriate, ask the students if they can think of similar incidents in their own lives or the lives of people they know. Ask them to describe what happened in those situations without divulging the names of the people involved. Encourage them to transfer learnings from one situation to another.

Sweet Revenge

Purpose:
To identify the moral values operating in a complex interpersonal situation; to recognize how values guide actions.

Materials:
one copy of *Sweet Revenge* for each student (optional)

Procedure:
You may read the story to the students, have them take turns reading, or distribute copies of the story and allow each student to read independently.

Ask the discussion questions, helping the students to identify the values inherent in the story, evaluate the motives and actions of the characters, and consider alternative courses of actions.

Discussion Questions:
1. What moral values played a part in this story?
2. Did Mr. Brickle show respect for the children who walked by his house? Did he show caring?
3. Did the children show respect for Mr. Brickle? How did they feel about him?
4. Was it right or wrong of Mr. Brickle to take James' bike?
5. Why did James' parents make him apologize to Mr. Brickle?
6. Was it right or wrong of the boys to plot to get even with Mr. Brickle?
7. How could the boys have handled their anger toward Mr. Brickle?
8. What do you think of the other boys for promising to stand by James and then running away instead?
9. Did James fake the other boys out? Did he guess that they would run away?
10. How would you have felt if you were James? What would you have done?

Sweet Revenge
by Thomas Pettepiece

"I dare you," Morey said.

James gulped. Morey had dared him before to do things at school, like ten pull-ups on the high bar, or hijack someone's ball during recess. Once he even dared him to stick out his tongue at the teacher while she wasn't looking, which he did, though he could have sworn she saw him at the last minute when she turned her head and his tongue retreated quickly into hiding.

Never had he felt such conflict. His stomach gurgled like an empty cavern. Beneath him he felt wobbly rubber legs, just like he saw on the Saturday morning cartoon characters. Morey, James, and three other boys were standing right below Mr. Brickle's big picture window, where Mr. Brickle stood every day after school and watched the children walk home. If he saw anyone goofing off, or bothering someone, or worst of all, stepping on his property in the slightest — on any part — the grass or the flower bed with chrysanthemum bulbs waiting for Spring, he would pound on the window and shake his fist at them. And if that didn't work, he would disappear from view for a moment, then reappear on the porch shouting, "You kids better stay out of the yard if you know what's good for you." No one ever really knew what would not be good for them if they didn't, but no one ever had the courage to defy the old man and find out. Until now that is.

All eyes were on James. The growing silence was starting to sound like cowardice in the face of pressure. "Come on James. Are you or aren't you?"

"Yeah. You're the one who's always talking so tough, saying 'Mr. Brickle is as dumb as a pickle,' and stuff like that. Are you going to throw that rock or not?"

James had wanted to for a long time, ever since Brickle had singled him out for parking his bike on the sidewalk in front of Brickle's house. James's dog had gotten loose, and James stopped his bike there so he could chase the mongrel on foot. When he came back the bike was gone. James didn't get it back for a week — not until he went over and apologized to Mr. Brickle, even though his parents said James didn't do anything wrong. The sidewalk was public property, they said. Still, Mr. Brickle or someone else could have tripped trying to go around the bike blocking the walkway.

That night after dinner, James and his buddies had met on the corner of Mr. Brickle's street and decided to get even with the old man by breaking his precious picture window. Then he couldn't stand there and stare at them anymore. Tonight was the perfect time, since, on their way home from school, they'd seen Mr. Brickle's son drive off with him. It was twilight, dark enough so the boys could not be seen crouching in the bushes beneath the window, but light enough that they were able to find the medium-size rock James now held in his hand.

"You're chicken, James," one of them said.

"All talk and no action," said another.

"You've got a yellow streak down your back longer than the highway," Morey blurted out.

"Well, you do it then, Big Mouth," James shot back.

"He didn't take my bike, man."

"Yeah, but he's yelled at you as much as me, calling you a punk kid and a juvenile delinquent."

The other boys murmured. It was true. Brickle had insulted them all at one time or another, and not one kid who walked by his house had been spared the wrath of his cruel words. Hadn't Mr. Brickle ever been a kid? What was wrong with him anyway?

"Well, James?" they all echoed in unison. "It's getting dark. Let's go. Now or never."

"Okay, okay. On one condition."

"What?" asked Morey.

""That we're all in this together. If anyone gets caught, we all get caught. And if anyone squeals, the rest will pound him. Got it?"

They all looked at each other for a moment, then back at James.

"Okay. Do it."

James stepped back so he could see the entire front of the house. It was an old wooden house, built over sixty years ago, with brick around the bottom. The section with the big window jutted out toward the street, so while it provided a perfect viewing stand for Mr. Brickle, it also made a perfect target.

James tossed the rock up and down in his palm, higher each time. He eyed the glass as though it were a bullseye on a shooting range. "Let's get Brickle, let's get Brickle," he began to chant. His arm was up in the air now, making circles as if he were preparing to throw the rock all the way to China. "Let's get Brickle," the other boys chanted with him. "Get Brickle, get Brickle, get Brickle," the rhythm continued as the boys spread out so they wouldn't get hit by huge chunks of glass from the enormous window.

"One, two..." James shouted.

"RUN!" cried Morey as they all scattered like squirrels fleeing a hunter.

"Three!"

But James held onto the rock, and then he just let it drop harmlessly to the ground. He turned away just in time to see the other boys disappear around a corner. James had made his decision.

Current Events Research

Purpose:
In this activity, the students select and summarize current-events articles dealing with important civic issues/events. Focusing on one problem, the students generate alternatives and achieve consensus on a solution to the problem.

Materials:
a news article about an issue or problem that clearly relates to the moral value of citizenship/civic virtue

Procedure:
A day or two before you lead this activity, ask the students to cut a current-events article from a newspaper or news magazine and bring it to school. Require that the articles deal with issues or events of civic importance. Bring an article of your own dealing with a problem for which creative solutions are obviously needed.

Talk to the students about the importance of being well-informed. Explain that the community, the nation, and the world are made up of individuals just like them. Communities are shaped by the interest and participation of individual people working together. People build, produce, feed, govern, and educate. In the process, they create conflicts and problems, which they also must solve. Ask the students what kinds of issues, events, and problems they discovered while reading the newspaper. Ask two or three volunteers to briefly tell the class about their articles.

Then ask all of the students to share their article with a partner. Allow about 5 minutes for this. Finally, read your article aloud to the class. Define terms used in the article, and discuss the problem. Ask these questions:
—What is the problem?
—Whose problem is it?
—What moral values are involved in this problem?

Announce that, through group discussion, the students are going to come up with solutions to the problem described in the article that you just read. Have the students form groups of three to five. Give the groups 1 minute to choose a leader and a recorder. Then announce that the groups will have 10 minutes to brainstorm solutions to the problem. If necessary, review the procedure for brainstorming.

Call time after 10 minutes, and have the groups discuss and evaluate their suggestions, one at a time. Their task is to choose one solution to present to the class. Suggest that they answer these questions:
—Will this solution solve the problem?
—Can this solution actually be done?
—Will combining any suggestions make a better solution?

Allow a few more minutes for discussion. Urge the groups to use the process of consensus-seeking to make their decision. Have the group leaders report the class. Then lead a culminating discussion.

Discussion Questions:
1. What was the hardest part about finding a solution to this problem? What was the easiest part?
2. If your group was not able to come to a decision, why not?
3. How were disagreements or conflicts handled in your group?
4. Is there any way for individuals or nations to avoid having problems? Explain.
5. How will learning to solve problems here in the classroom help prepare us to solve them in the outside world?

Being the Very Best Me

Purpose:
To examine personal decisions that were made based on moral values.

Materials:
writing and drawing materials

Procedure:
Begin by reviewing the universal moral values examined so far by the students. Write a list on the board, e.g.:
Trustworthiness
Respect
Responsibility
Justice and Fairness
Caring
Citizenship

In your own words, explain one of the following assignments:

1. I want you to think of an <u>ethical</u> (values) <u>dilemma</u> from your own life. Perhaps you had to make a decision that involved one of the values on the board. For example, maybe you knew that the decision would cause someone to either trust you or not trust you in the future. Or perhaps the decision involved taking responsibility for some action, or being fair in the way you judged a situation. Most of us face moral dilemmas from time to time. Once you have identified the dilemma, write about it. Describe the circumstances, what your choices were, and explain how you resolved the problem and why. If this dilemma is still going on now, describe how you are feeling about it and what you might do. If you'd rather, you may draw a picture of the situation — or you may both write and draw.

2. Your assignment is to describe in writing a behavior that you've <u>changed</u> based on moral grounds. Perhaps you used to tease certain people because of things about them that were different, and you've stopped doing that because it's wrong. Or maybe you used to cheat occasionally, but have decided to start taking responsibility for your own work. Have you become more honest? Trustworthy? Considerate of others? Why did you decide to make this change? Describe the change, what led up to it, and how it feels to have strengthened your character. If you'd rather, you may draw two pictures — one showing the old behavior and another illustrating the new behavior. Or you may both write and draw.

Have the students share their papers in groups of three to five. Allow plenty of time for discussion. Give the students an opportunity to correct and rewrite their papers before placing the papers, along with illustrations, in a binder.

Discussion Questions:
1. *What causes certain decisions to become difficult dilemmas?*
2. *What kind of questions can you ask yourself when you have a tough decision to make?*
3. *Was it hard to make the change you described?*
4. *How do you feel now about the decision or change you made?*

A Game of Ethics

Purpose:
To have students acknowledge each other and themselves for ethical behaviors and to identify specific behavior associated with four universal moral values.

Materials:
one copy of the experience sheet, *Ethics Bingo!*, and a pen/pencil for each student

Procedure:
Use this activity as a warm-up or energizer, and to help the students focus on ethical behavior in the context of four universal moral values — honesty, respect, responsibility, and kindness.

Distribute the bingo sheets and explain to the students that they are to mill about, interviewing their classmates, in an effort to find someone to sign each square on their sheet.

Depending on the size of the group, limit the number of times a particular student's signature may appear on each sheet. For example, if ten students are playing, you may wish to allow students to sign the same sheet up to three times. If twenty are playing, the limit might be two times; thirty might be limited to one signing per sheet.

Instruct the students to talk to each other about the items on their sheets. For example, if a student says she "did a favor for someone recently," find out what the favor was and for whom it was done.

Conclude the activity with a follow-up discussion.

Discussion Questions:
1. *Were any squares particularly hard to fill? Which ones?*
2. *Which squares were the easiest to fill?*
3. *What are ethics?*
4. *What is one word that describes all of the behaviors listed on the sheet?*
5. *Do you think it's possible to learn to do all of these things, all of the time? Why or why not?*

Variation:
Distribute the bingo sheets, but instead of having the students fill them out in class, stipulate that they may be completed only during recess and lunch breaks. Give the students one or two days to get their signatures.

Ethics Bingo!

Get someone to sign your sheet who:

Respect	Kindness
says "please" and "thank you"	hugged someone today
says "excuse me"	appreciates others
is a good listener	did a favor for someone recently
is usually on time	writes letters to friends or relatives
settles conflicts peacefully	complimented someone today
throws away litter	makes cards or gifts to give to others
accepts people's differences	calls a grandparent just to say hello

Honesty	Responsibility
returned a lost item	cares for a pet
hasn't cheated on a test this year	makes own bed
tells the truth	always follows rules and obeys laws
kept a promise this week	is a good role model for young children
stands up for friends and family	did all his/her homework this week
never asks a friend to do something wrong	admits mistakes
always returns borrowed things	controls his/her temper

Values Affect Decisions

Purpose:
To have students evaluate their own and others' behaviors, discuss how values and ethics are formed, and to explain the difference between thinking about and doing something bad.

Materials:
chalkboard; chart paper, marking pens, masking tape, and three signs prepared prior to the session (see "Procedure")

Procedure:
Ask the students if they know what the term ethics means. Write the word on the board, listen to any ideas that the students voice, and clarify that ethics are principles or values having to do with right and wrong.

Ask the students: *Who can tell us about something you've done in the last few days that was a good thing to do?*

Call on volunteers. After each person shares, ask him or her: How did you know that what you did was a good thing to do?

Discuss various ways of knowing: because it feels good, because parents have said it's good, because anything else would feel bad, etc.

Next, ask the students: *Who is willing to tell us about a bad thing you've done recently?*

Again, ask each volunteer: *How do you know that what you did was bad?*

Be sure to take a turn yourself and share something that you're not proud of having done. Emphasize that all people do bad things at times. That doesn't mean that they are bad people, only that they made a mistake. The most important thing is to recognize and admit that you've done something wrong and learn from the experience.

Place these three signs (prepared ahead of time) on the wall:

- I think that was a very good thing to do.
- I'm not sure whether it was good or bad.
- I think that was a very bad thing to do.

Tell the students that you are going to read them some situations. They are to go and stand in front of the sign that matches what they think or feel about the behavior of the <u>principal person</u> in the situation.

One at a time, read the situations from the list on the following page. Give the students time to decide and position themselves. Then walk up to each group and ask individual students, "Why are you standing here?"

Interview the students about their reasons for deciding the way they did. Underscore examples that demonstrate different perceptions of what happened in the situation. When values have played a clear role in someone's decision, discuss with the class how values are developed.

Have the students return to their seats. Conclude the activity with a general discussion.

Discussion Questions:
1. *What's the difference between having a bad thought or feeling, and actually doing a bad thing?*
2. *When you find yourself thinking about doing something bad, how do you stop yourself from doing it?*
3. *How do we learn the difference between good and bad, right and wrong?*
4. *If you know that a friend is about to do something bad, should you try to stop him or her? Why or why not?*
5. *How about just saying, "It's not my problem" and not worrying about it?*

Extension:
Consider spreading the various parts of this activity over two or three days. Then spend more time examining each part: good behaviors; bad behaviors; the role of values and perceptions; the differences between thinking/feeling and doing; and how ethics are developed.

Situations

- Keith beats up a younger boy because he overhears the boy call his sister a bad name.

- Without asking, Maria borrows an old ring of her mother's. When she loses it, Maria decides not to say anything. Chances are her mother won't notice that the ring is missing for a long, long time.

- Willie is in a big hurry to get home. He can't see any cars in either direction so he crosses on the red signal.

- Linda sees a girl she doesn't like cheating on a spelling test, so she tells the teacher.

- Linda sees her friend cheating on a social studies quiz, and doesn't say anything to anyone.

- Sandie overhears the teacher scolding two classmates for leaving a mess on the work table. Sandie helped make the mess, but she doesn't speak up.

- Three tough kids are making fun of a new student. Reginald is a little afraid of the tough kids, but he stands up for the new student anyway, telling the tough kids to get lost.

- Jon stays up very late watching old movies and can barely move the next morning. He decides to stay home from school and get some sleep.

- Roberto finishes his homework early, so he helps his younger brother with his homework.

- Jeanne knows that Mr. Snipes hates to have kids cut across his lawn, but she also knows that Mr. Snipes is on vacation, so she cuts across anyway.

What Would You Do?

Purpose:
The students will determine ethical behaviors for typical self-interest situations and identify the underlying moral values in each situation.

Materials
one copy of the experience sheet, *Decision Point!*, for each small group; pencils/pens

Procedure:
Introduce the concepts of *self-interest* and *self-protection*. Point out that most of us know the difference between right and wrong. We often know exactly what we *should* do in a situation, even though we don't always do it. When we desire something for ourselves, we often let that desire get into a fight with our knowledge about what is right and wrong. Sometimes self-interest wins.

Have the students form groups of four or five. Give each group a copy of the experience sheet and go over the directions. In your own words, elaborate:

Take turns reading the situations aloud in your group. After a situation is read, brainstorm ideas about what the person in the situation should do. Have a recorder write down all the ideas. When the group runs out of ideas, go around the circle and take turns saying what you as an individual would do if you were in that situation.

In a follow-up discussion, focus on the moral values underlying each situation. Emphasize that when these moral values get into contests with self-interest, the moral values should always be the winners. Do not equivocate on this point.

Discussion Questions:
1. *Which moral value are you breaking when you steal? (Honesty)*
2. *What moral values are you breaking if you treat someone badly just because he or she is different? (Respect/Kindness)*
3. *What moral values are you breaking when you keep something that doesn't belong to you? (Honesty/Responsibility)*
4. *What moral value are you breaking if you blame someone else (or allow someone to get blamed) for something you did? (Honesty/Responsibility/Respect)*
5. *Why are decisions like these sometimes hard to make?*
6. *How does making the right decisions help you become a good person?*

EXPERIENCE SHEET

Decision Point!

Take one situation at a time. Read it aloud and talk about it with your group. Make a list of the things you think the person in the situation should do. Then go around the group and take turns answering the question, "What would *you* do?"

1. Norman likes many toys, especially cars. At the toy store, he sees a car he has wanted for a long time, but it costs too much money. He looks around and sees that no one is watching. He could easily slip the car into his pocket. *What should Norman do?*

2. Lisa comes out to lunch late and sees her friends making fun of a new girl. Lisa likes the new girl and thinks that her friends should not make fun of her just because she is new. She wants to be with her friends because she likes them, but doesn't like to be mean. *What should Lisa do?*

3. Trahn finds a wallet on the ground. Inside is a twenty dollar bill — just enough money to buy his mother something nice for her birthday. Trahn knows he should return the wallet, but he wants to surprise his mom. *What should Trahn do?*

4. Shelly cracks the glass on her mother's computer monitor. She cracks it with her little sister's bat, which she isn't supposed to be using in the house. If she gets in trouble she won't be able to go to her friend's birthday party. She could easily blame it on her sister. *What should Shelly do?*

5. Eric's mom made a tray of fresh brownies. Those are Eric's favorite. His mom says that Eric can have only two. When Eric finishes his two brownies, he sees the plate sitting on the counter by itself and his mom isn't around. Eric really wants more brownies. *What should Eric do?*

6. Rosa and her best friend get in a fight. Rosa really wants to make up, but her friend won't talk to her. Rosa knows that she did something mean and wants to apologize, but her friend did something mean, too. *What should Rosa do?*

Dilemmas by the Dozen

Purpose:
To identify moral values underlying the decisions of children and adults in ordinary situations; to recognize how values guide actions.

Materials:
copies of the dilemmas for distribution (optional, depending on method of implementation)

Procedure:
These stories/dilemmas may be used in several ways. Here are three suggestions:

• Occasionally read a dilemma aloud to the students. Ask the discussion questions. Help the students to identify the values inherent in the situation, evaluate the motives and actions of the characters, and consider alternative courses of actions.

• Divide the class into small groups, and give each group a copy of one dilemma (including discussion questions). Have the groups read and discuss their dilemma, answering the questions. Ask each group in turn to summarize its dilemma and conclusions for the rest of the class.

• Divide the class into small groups, and give each group a copy of one dilemma. Have each group develop, rehearse, and deliver a role play of its dilemma for the rest of the class. After each role play, ask the discussion questions, allowing the entire class to respond. Brainstorm alternative actions in each situation and ask the performing group to role play one or two of those.

Larry is supposed to meet Paul and Robert for a frisbee game at the park. Just as he is about to leave, he receives a phone call from Manny. Manny is studying for the math test tomorrow and sounds very confused and worried. He asks Larry to come over and help him. Larry and Manny are good friends, so Larry doesn't want to upset Manny, but he doesn't want to miss the game either. He decides to tell Manny that he has to go somewhere with his parents.

The next morning at school, Paul tells Manny that he missed a good frisbee game the previous afternoon, and he mentions that Larry was there. Manny feels hurt and angry. During the math test, he tries to copy off of Larry's paper.

Discussion Questions:
1. What are the moral values in this situation?
2. How would you feel if you were Larry?
3. What could Larry handle the situation?
4. How would you feel if you were Manny?
5. What could Manny do?

The Dennis family lives atop a hill at the end of a long, steep winding driveway. The lot is large and tree covered. One evening, when Mr. Dennis pulls up the driveway and parks his car, he forgets to put on the emergency brake. Almost immediately, the car begins to inch backwards toward the slope. During the night it crosses the edge of the driveway, picks up momentum, rolls down the hill and crashes into a tree on the edge of the Henry's yard. The car is a total loss and the Mr. and Mrs. Henry are angry about the tree, which they insist is going to die. Mr. Dennis explains what happened and apologizes. He cleans up the mess and suggests everyone wait to see if the tree recovers. But the Henrys demand to be paid immediately for the damage. Reluctantly, Mrs. Dennis calls the insurance company, which pays Mr. and Mrs. Henry $7,000 — the cost to replace the tree with a similar full-grown shade tree. Weeks pass, and the original tree not only recovers — it looks healthier than ever. The Henrys keeps the $7,000 and, when Mr. and Mrs. Dennis renew their insurance policy, they discover that the accident has caused their rates to increase. The two families quit speaking to each other.

Discussion Questions:
1. What are the moral values in this situation?
2. Who is responsible for what?
3. What is right about the way this situation was handled? What is wrong?
3. If you were Mr. and Mrs. Dennis, how would you feel? What would you do?
5. If you were Mr. and Mrs. Henry, how would you feel? What would you do?
4. Did the insurance company do the right thing?

Julie has a plan to create an elaborate science project that she is sure will win the big science-fair prize. She gets started, but quickly runs into problems, so he asks Liz to be her partner. Both are good science students, but Liz is especially good at solving problems and building things. On the day of the science fair, Liz is sick, so Julie sets everything up and demonstrates the project by herself. Sure enough, the project wins first prize. When Julie is interviewed by reporters, she doesn't give any credit to Liz. In fact, she never mentions that she had a partner at all. She answers every question with, "I did this," or "I did that." When Liz sees Julie's picture in the paper and reads the article, she feels bad. But she never says anything to Julie.

Discussion Questions:

1. What are the moral values in this situation?
2. If you were Liz, how would you feel? What would you do?
3. How do you think Julie feels? How should she feel? What should she do?
4. What would you like to see happen in this situation?

On Saturday, Ms. Hornaday goes to Lacy's department store and buys $200 worth of holiday gifts for her family and friends. On this shopping day only, the store is offering one $10 gift certificate for every $100 a customer spends. Before leaving the store, Ms. Hornaday shows her receipts to the customer service clerk and receives two gift certificates, which she can use to buy $20 worth of merchandise. Later, at home, Ms. Hornaday decides that some of the gifts were poor choices. The next day, she returns half of the items. The store accepts her returns and refunds her money, but Ms. Hornaday keeps — and plans to use — both gift certificates.

Discussion Questions:

1. What are the moral values in this situation?
2. If you were Ms. Hornaday, what would you do with the gift certificates? Why?

Maria and Colleen are walking home together on a particularly hot afternoon. When they get to Maria's house, Colleen says goodbye and continues down the block. Suddenly, she hears Maria calling after her, "Hey, how about a swim in my pool?" Colleen hesitates. A swim would feel wonderful, but Colleen knows that Maria's parents are both at work. Even Maria isn't supposed to swim unsupervised, let alone a friend of Maria's. They could both get in a lot of trouble.

When Colleen tells Maria about her fears, Maria says, "Don't worry, no one will find out. On a day like this, everything will dry off real fast — including us. Come on!"

Colleen gives in, and the two girls head for the pool. When Colleen gets home, her mother asks why she is late. Colleen says that she stayed after school to help the teacher.

Discussion Questions:

1. What are the moral values in this situation?
2. Why do Maria's parents have a rule against swimming without supervision?
3. What are Maria's responsibilities in this situation? What are Colleen's?

Mr. Escobar takes his car to the garage for a smog test and certificate. The car fails the test and the mechanic tells Mr. Escobar that the necessary repairs will cost $60. Mr. Escobar has heard about a man who will fake a smog certificate for $20. Several of Mr. Escobar's coworkers have gone to this man, rather then have their cars fixed. Mr. Escobar wonders if he should go, too.

Discussion Questions:
1. What are the moral values in this situation?
2. If a lot of people get fake smog certificates, what are the consequences?
3. Who is breaking the law in this situation?
4. What do you think Mr. Escobar should do?
5. Does anyone have a moral obligation to report the man who is faking smog certificates? Who and why?

When Mr. and Mrs. Greer go on vacation for three weeks, they ask Kim to feed their cat, Sydney, twice a day. They also ask her to water their yard and houseplants. They offer to pay Kim $10 a week and she agrees. Every morning before school, Kim stops by the Greer house. Sydney is always waiting for his breakfast near the back door. In the evening, she returns, feeds the cat his dinner, and checks to see if anything needs watering. For the first two weeks, Kim sticks to this routine. However, during the third week, Kim herself has vacation from school and sleeps later than usual. On Monday and Tuesday, she doesn't get around to feeding Sydney his breakfast until 10:00 a.m. and forgets to check the plants. On Wednesday, she stops briefly at noon before rushing off to a friend's house. On Thursday, Kim goes to a movie in the evening and forgets to feed the cat his dinner. When she goes over on Friday morning, Sydney isn't at the back door and doesn't answer her call. Friday evening, Sydney is in the yard, but doesn't seem hungry.

When the Greers arrive home on Sunday, they pay Kim and ask how everything went. She tells them, "Fine." On Monday evening, the Greers phone and ask Kim to come next door and answer some questions. They ask Kim why Sydney showed up hungry at another neighbor's house several times during the previous week, and why two of their favorite house plants are dry and wilted. Kim acts surprised and tells them she has no idea why. She insists that she did everything they asked her to do.

Discussion Questions:
1. What are the moral values in this situation?
2. What do Kim's actions say about her?
3. How did Kim's actions affect the cat? ...the plants? ...the Greers? ...Kim?
4. What should Kim have done?

An employer mismanages his company and is frequently late paying his workers. Robert, an employee of the company, decides he's had enough and plans to quit. He tries to collect his back pay before announcing his resignation, but the employer still owes him $2,000. Robert comes up with a plan: Before turning in his key, he will go to the office at night and remove the computer from his desk. The computer, worth about $2,000, does not belong to Robert, but he is the only one who uses it.

Discussion Questions:
1. *What are the moral values in this situation?*
2. *What are the employer's responsibilities?*
3. *What are Robert's responsibilities?*
4. *What's wrong with Robert's plan?*
5. *How would you feel if you were Robert and never knew whether or not you were going to be paid? What would you do?*
6. *How would you feel if you were the employer and one of your workers left with equipment that belonged to you? What would you do?*

Louis heads down the street to see if Jimmy wants to do some skateboarding. He finds his friend in the garage sorting piles of newspapers, cans, and bottles. "That's no fun. Can't you do it later?" urges Louis.

"No," answers Jimmy. "I have to finish getting this stuff ready for Mom and me to take to the recycling center."

"Why don't you just throw it away?" asks Louis. "The trash collector is coming tomorrow."

"Because if we throw it in the trash, it will go to the landfill," answers Jimmy, "and if we take to the recycling center, it won't. It'll be used again. Don't you collect things for recycling at your house?"

"No," shrugs Louis. He unwraps a candy bar and starts eating it.

"Why?" asks Jimmy.

"I don't know. Too much trouble I guess."

Louis heads his skateboard back out to the street. "See you later," he calls, coasting smoothly onto the pavement.

Jimmy looks up from his work just in time to see Louis throw the candy wrapper into the gutter. He opens his mouth to yell, but Louis was already halfway down the block. Jimmy sighs and shakes his head. Then he walks out to the curb and picks up the candy wrapper.

Discussion Questions:
1. What are the moral values in this situation?
2. What do the actions of the two boys say about them?
3. How can people show respect for the environment?

Newt doesn't have enough money to pay his rent. After several weeks of unemployment, he has just started a new job and has not been paid yet. The landlord telephones and asks when he can expect a check. Newt plans to move to a cheaper house next month, but is afraid to tell the landlord. He thinks about lying, just to keep the landlord off his back. He figures it will take the landlord a few weeks to evict him, during which time he can save his money for a new place. But the landlord has always been cooperative and nice, and Newt feels guilty taking advantage of him. Newt wonders what will happen if he tells the truth. If the landlord kicks him out, Newt has nowhere to go.

Discussion Questions:
1. What moral values are involved in this situation?
2. How do you think the landlord feels?
3. If you were Newt, how would you feel? What would you do?

On Saturday, Bud and Holly stop by the library to turn in some books and see Mai working alone at a back table. They walk over to say hello.

"What are you working on Mai?" asks Holly.

"I decided to enter the Flag Day essay contest," answers Mai. "The winning essay will be printed in the newspaper. That would be a great honor. Are you going to enter?"

"No," says Holly.

"I haven't given it much thought," responds Bud. "What are you writing about?"

"The meaning of the flag," answers Mai. "It's a little hard because I haven't lived in this country very long. Maybe you can help me. What does it mean to you?"

"I don't know," answers Holly. "But we say a pledge to the flag."

"I haven't given it much thought," responds Bud. "But last year at school, I helped put the flag up and take it down."

"What about liberty and justice?" asks Mai. "Those words are in the pledge. Don't they mean anything to you?"

"Oh, sure they do," shrugs Holly.

"I haven't thought much about it," says Bud. "But this is sure a boring way to spend a Saturday. Why don't you come to the movies with us instead."

Mai thinks for a minute, then smiles and says, "Thank you. But I must write. In the country where I used to live, we didn't always have the liberty to choose what we wanted to do on Saturday. And if there was an essay contest, all students had to enter. They didn't have the liberty to refuse. If they refused, their whole family could be punished. In the United States, I can choose to write — or not to write. I like that. That is liberty and justice."

As Holly and Bud start to leave, Mai calls softly after them, "Thank you for helping me with my essay. You gave me some great ideas."

Discussion Questions:
1. What are the moral values in this situation?
2. If you were Holly or Bud, how would you feel about Mai?
3. What does Mai like about living in the United States?
4. What can Holly and Bud learn from Mai's example?

Kurt enjoys riding his bike to school the morning after a storm. Sometimes he flies fast down the wet streets, sending spray up on all sides. Other times he navigates between the puddles, wheeling this way and that like an infantryman avoiding land mines. This morning, he nearly makes it to school without becoming a casualty. When he loses his traction and goes down a block away, everything gets wet, including the adventure comic book Sergio loaned him the day before. It is soaked and muddy.

Kurt feels terrible. He explains what happened as he hands the book to Sergio. "I'm really sorry," he apologizes. "I should have been more careful."

Sergio looks upset for a moment and Kurt is afraid he has made his friend very angry. Then Sergio sighs and says, "It's okay. The same thing could have happened to me."

Kurt feels relieved. He tells himself that he will never be so careless with someone else's property again.

That afternoon, when Kurt opens the door to his bedroom, he is greeted by a squeal from his four-year-old brother. Kenny is hiding something behind his back.

"What are you doing in here?" asks Kurt accusingly. "And what's that behind your back."

"Nothing," says Kenny weakly, tears rising in his eyes.

Kurt lunges forward, grabs Kenny by the arm and turns him around. Kenny is holding Kurt's newest model spacecraft, and it is broken.

"I'm sorry," wails Kenny. "I was just looking at it and it dropped. Don't be mad, Kurt!"

Kurt stares at the shattered hull and feels his temper flare. Then he remembers the comic book and Sergio's reaction. He sets his books on the bed, takes a deep breath, and gently tussles Kenny's hair. "Don't cry, Ken," he says. "We all make mistakes sometimes. Let's see if we can fix it."

Discussion Questions:
1. What are the moral values in this situation?
2. How would you feel if you were Sergio? What would you do?
3. What did Kurt learn from Sergio's reaction?
4. Have you ever forgiven someone for hurting you or one of your possessions? Explain.
5. Why is it a good idea to forgive sometimes?
6. Do you think Kurt and Kenny will make the same mistakes again? Why or why not?

Unit 8
Service Learning

Through service learning, students participate in deliberate character-building experiences — systematic activities that result in real assistance to others, as well as personal growth. In the process, those activities reinforce specific values, such as responsibility, caring, and citizenship.

Many pro-social activities can be carried out by students in schools at all levels. Participating in service learning gives students opportunities to practice moral values and develop good character. Schools with many extracurricular activities and service opportunities almost always do a better job of developing student character.

Service learning programs should include:

- Training. Students who have never helped others may not know how. Train them in basic helping skills.
- Supervision. Help students adjust to new situations and continue to develop needed skills, while providing feedback, encouragement, and motivation to continue.
- Ongoing support. Provide help with problem solving, encourage reflection, continue to motivate, and give plenty of recognition.

Classroom Service Opportunities
    aides
    messengers
    monitors
    clean-up helpers
    tutors
    homework buddies
    members of cooperative learning projects

School Service Opportunities
- competitive sports
- performing groups — band, choir, dramatics, forensics
- fundraising
- school newspaper
- student council
- academic competitions
- school greeters and tour guides
- conflict mediators
- safety patrol

Community Service Opportunities
- building projects
- community clean-up projects
- recycling/re-use centers
- day-care centers
- retirement and nursing home visitations
- at-home assistance for elderly

A School Service Project

Purpose
For the students to identify the needs and desires of new students and to creatively compile information and services to meet the needs of new students.

Materials:
multiple copies of an appropriate organizer, e.g., inexpensive 3-ring binders, expandable file folders, large envelopes, presentation folders with pockets, etc.; art materials

Procedure:
Begin this activity by asking the students: *What is it like to be a new kid at school? How many of you have had that experience?*

Invite volunteers to share what it's like to enter a new school where you don't know anyone. Ask them if anyone showed them around during the first week or so, and whether or not the staff and students were welcoming and friendly. Point out that one of the nicest things they can do is to make a new student feel a part of the school from the very first day.

Announce that, as a service project, the students are going to prepare "survival kits" to give to new students.

As a total group, brainstorm the contents of the kit. Try to think of as many things as possible that a new student might find useful or encouraging. Follow the rules of brainstorming, i.e., anything goes, be creative, no evaluation during the brainstorming process, no put downs of any kind. Your list might include:
- a map of the school
- information about the school (description, history, unique characteristics, special relationships, e.g., with local colleges or businesses)
- a school district telephone directory (perhaps an abbreviated version)
- a school calendar, with special events marked
- a student handbook or list of rules/requirements
- information about teachers (names, classes, room numbers)
- information about office staff
- lists of sports, service groups, and clubs, with information on how they are organized and how to become involved
- descriptions of future school events, including dates and times
- location of lost and found
- jokes, cartoons, or stories authored by students

- student-made coupons redeemable for special services, e.g., a campus tour, help with homework, introductions to six kids, a recess game partner, etc.
- a copy of the student newspaper
- PTA information
- a map of the town or city
- names and telephone numbers of local medical facilities
- coupons for treats at local stores and businesses
- information about public transportation
- a candy bar or treat

After the brainstorming process is concluded, go back and evaluate the list, narrow it down and make final selections.

Choose teams of volunteers to obtain or prepare the various items needed. When everything has been collected, appoint an "assembly team" to:
1. Decide on the best presentation of the items.
2. Put together a model kit
3. Design and produce a cover
3. Develop a system for efficiently assembling the kits.

Appoint another team to answer distribution questions. Have them consider the pros and cons of several distribution alternatives. For example:
- Assign a person to hand deliver each kit and perhaps act as a companion/guide throughout the first day.
- Mail the kit.
- Deliver the kit to the home of the new student.
- Give out kits at a monthly "newcomers" reception or party.

When the kits are finished and all of the decisions regarding distribution have been made, facilitate a culminating discussion.

Discussion Questions:
1. *How do you feel when you do something to help a person you don't yet know?*
2. *How would you feel if a friendly student presented you with a kit like this when you entered a new school?*
3. *How do we benefit from reaching out to others?*

A Community Service Activity

Purpose:
For the students to create and assemble gifts for seniors in managed-care environments and to spend time with the recipients of the gift baskets created.

Materials:
a variety of gift items; suitable containers; wrapping and decorating materials

Procedure:
This is a perfect activity for the holidays, but is needed and appreciated all year long.

Have the students research the nursing homes, senior centers, and retirement homes in your area. Ask them to find out:
—the number of residents
—the general health of residents
—recreational and personal-care needs
—whether the administration would welcome visits and gifts from children
—the best times of the day for visits

Based on this information, choose the most compatible senior residence. Then telephone that organization and obtain more specific suggestions concerning what to include in gift baskets. If the resident population is greater than the number of baskets you plan to make, ask the administrator to select individuals who especially need and would appreciate the service. If possible, obtain a list of names so that the students can label the baskets. Calendar a date and time for the class to visit.

Prepare the baskets. Finalize a list of items. Possibilities include:
- personal grooming supplies (combs, brushes, toothpaste, shampoo, deodorant, mirrors, lipstick)
- food (fruit, nuts, candy, muffins, cookies, breads)
- clothing
- sheets, pillowcases, or blankets
- flowers (potted plants, silk arrangements, fresh)
- letters and cards
- videos, audio tapes and compact disks (used CDs are very inexpensive and never wear out)
- books

Decide what kind of container will best hold the contents of the gift baskets. You may use actual baskets (natural or synthetic) or you may find that boxes, gift bags, or bags that the students decorate themselves work better.

Hold a fund-raiser to raise money for the gifts, or circulate a flyer describing the project and listing of needed items. Ask students and staff members to contribute one new item.

Have teams of students assemble the gift baskets and wrap or decorate them.

Talk to the senior organization to find out what other activities the students can do with the residents during their visit. For example, they might:
—perform a skit
—lead some sing-a-longs
—play games
—lead simple stretching and movement exercises
—teach the seniors a dance (wheelchairs can dance, too)

Brief the students about appropriate behavior during their visit. In particular, make them aware of the physical limitations of the people they'll be visiting, and share any specific guidelines provided by the administrator of the senior residence.

After the visit, lead the class in a follow-up discussion.

Discussion Questions:
1. *What was the best part of this activity for you?*
2. *How did giving to the seniors cause you to feel? How do you think the seniors felt?*
3. *Would you like to visit the center again? What ideas do you have for another visit?*

Extension:
Be ready to sponsor an "Adopt a Senior" or "Adopt a Grandfriend" program for students who respond particularly well to this activity. Turn a single visit into a long-term commitment by each student to visit, share, and support one particular senior.

If your heart is in Social-Emotional Learning, visit us online.

Come see us at
www.InnerchoicePublishing.com

Our web site gives you a look at all our other Social-Emotional Learning-based books, free activities, articles, research, and learning and teaching strategies. Every week you'll get a new Sharing Circle topic and lesson.

15079 Oak Chase Court
Wellington, FL 33414

www.ingramcontent.com/pod-product-compliance
Lightning Source LLC
Chambersburg PA
CBHW080452170426
43196CB00016B/2770